Mindset
Mastery

Sending Miracles

Louise Presley-Turner

Louise

x

Mindset Mastery

www.gameoflife.com

ISBN 978-1-907308-12-3

First Published in Great Britain in 2014 by Compass Publishing.

Printed in Great Britain by Berforts Information Press.

Set and laid out by The Book Refinery Ltd.

To Jean and Laura, I love you!

"Those who don't believe in magic, will never find it."
~ Roald Dahl

Contents

Contents

Acknowledgements

My second book has been a long time coming. But I'm thrilled that it's finally here and I hope you love the result.

Firstly, I'd like to thank you, my reader, for having the willingness and courage to change your life. It's a privilege to take this journey with you and I wish you many, many miracles along the way.

As always, I'd like to thank my rock, Carl, for his unwavering support and belief in me. I'm not always the easiest wife to live with ;)

I'd like to thank my gorgeous children, Esme and Elliott, for keeping my feet well and truly on the ground. And my doggy Max for keeping my toes warm as I typed away. I love you all, always.

I'd like to thank my mum and sister for being my cheerleaders, and my dad for always believing in my writing ability. And I'd like to thank my wise old grandma Edith for shining a light on my spiritual path. I love you all.

I'd like to thank my good friend and spiritual guru, Alison Ward; our many conversations have helped me immensely. Thank you also to my editor, Danielle Wrate, and my typesetter, Alexa Whitten. You've both helped to make my book shine.

But above all I'd like to thank my angels for their guidance and love. I live a very blessed life on planet earth and I wouldn't be where I am today without my heavenly support team. Thank you always and forever.

Prologue

I spent the first 25 years of my life looking for something that I couldn't name, understand or articulate. From a very young age, I felt a deep calling within, which I couldn't comprehend. I knew that I was somehow different from my peers. I was an old soul who could feel people's pain, and I was heavily influenced by the energies of those around me. School was a real challenge for me because the traditional academic system didn't support my learning style. I spent most of my younger years floundering and trying to keep my head above the muddy waters. Most of the time I felt like I was drowning. One teacher even told my mother, *"She's a lovely girl, but I don't think she'll ever be a high flyer!"* After constantly being told that I wasn't quite good enough, I walked out into the world, aged 16, feeling like a fraud. I thought that I had to conceal the awful truth about my inadequacies. And I know that my story is not unique.

In a constant bid to prove to the world that I was good enough, I had a steely determination to prove my worth. Highly ambitious and highly competitive, I worked hard at whatever I put my mind to. I was the kind of kid who always had to put in way more effort than everyone else, and I often looked at my peers with real envy as they completed their work with ease. I would spend weeks and weeks revising for an exam, yet I would still fail miserably. I could double check my assignments over and over yet still be downgraded for my poor grammar and spelling. I felt like I didn't meet the mark. I didn't fit the mould and I was a disappointment. I didn't believe in myself and I ran away from the world of academia as fast as I could.

When I was a child, my mother would always push me out front. She would encourage me to ask for things in shops, articulate myself to strangers and make new friends wherever I went. My mum gave me the strength to forge my own way through the jungle of life, and this made me a very strong, independent and reliable girl. This was a huge blessing as it made me a confident youngster with a charm and innocence that people often found endearing. People took me under their wing in a bid to protect and nurture me. But this innocence and charm was a cloak of disguise, because I truly believed that if people knew who I really was, they would be as disappointed as my teachers and parents. It was a big burden to carry.

As I progressed into adulthood, I looked to my peers to help me define myself. I compared myself to my friends, wanted what they had and wore what they wore. I was a sheep. I married and bought a house at the tender age of 22. By 25, I was a marketing manager for a large automotive brand and had just become a mother to my beautiful daughter. I had crammed a lot into my 25 years. But the more I achieved, the more lost I felt. Something didn't add up.

I remember one evening lying in the bath and having a horrible, scary thought. As I looked back at my life, I realised that I had already done more than most people do in a lifetime. I'd travelled, started a challenging career, married, bought a house, possessed lovely material things and had a baby... but all these wonderful things still hadn't filled the mysterious void in my life. I was desperately looking for something, but how can you find something when you haven't a clue what you're looking for? I felt desperate. I felt lost. I had no idea what was missing, but clearly sometime big was amiss.

When my daughter was six-months-old, I returned to work and resumed my old identity in the corporate world. But something had shifted inside of me. I was a mother now and having a baby really does rock your world and change the landscape of your life. I recall one my closest colleagues bounding into my office one morning in her normal bright, cheery way. She was waving a rather bright yellow book under my nose called *'Excuse Me, Your Life is Waiting'* by Lynn Grabhorn. She had read it while on holiday and told me how amazing and life changing it was. Immediately, it was apparent to me that this was some kind of self-help book, and I wasn't particularly interested having never read anything in this genre before. But not wanting to pour cold water on her enthusiasm, I took the book and promised I'd take a look. It sat on my kitchen worktop for weeks before guilt and obligation overtook me enough to pick it up.

I sat down one evening and started reading. Just a few pages in, I was captivated. No other book had grabbed me like this. Its content resonated within me deeply. I felt a connection, I felt alive and I felt a truth rising through me. This was something that I had never experienced before. I knew that I had opened the door to a new world. This was the catalyst to my transformation. A switch had been flicked and a doorway had opened. There was no going back.

In the months that followed, I surrounded myself with books on quantum physics, neuroscience, self-love, metaphysics, psychology and angels. I was hungry for knowledge, and I had never felt this way about anything in my life. A deep burning passion was roaring inside me and each new book fuelled my fire more. I hadn't a clue where all this new information was leading me, but I knew that it was guiding me somewhere. I realised that I was on the brink of something really big. Meanwhile, my husband and family were watching from afar and my shift was making them very uncomfortable. The girl who loved nothing better than to curl up on the sofa with a trashy novel was now devouring books on quantum mechanics. I could understand their apprehension!

Six months into my journey, something totally transformational happened. In the early hours of a very normal Wednesday morning in 2006, I was awoken by a very strange experience that's really quite hard to describe. As I lay there in a light morning slumber, something inside of me started shouting the numbers 555 very loudly. The experience was so intense that I immediately shot up in bed. The numbers 555 were repeatedly ringing in my ears. It wasn't an external sound, but something coming from inside me. Stunned, I looked across at my husband who was still sound asleep. I then settled back down and tried to make sense of my experience. Unable to, I shuffled out of bed to go to the toilet. In a complete daze, I walked back from the bathroom to my bed. And, as I glanced over at the alarm clock, I could clearly see that it read 5.55am! Well, this was too much of a coincidence for me to ignore. I lay back down on the bed, my head racing, desperately looking for logical reasons for what had just happened. I couldn't find any!

I remembered reading Doreen Virtue's book 'Angel Numbers', so I decided to see if I could find out what the numbers 555 represented.

Here's what I found out about this number sequence:

'Buckle your seatbelts. A major life change is upon you. This change should not be viewed as being 'positive' or 'negative' since all change is but a natural part of life's flow. Perhaps this change is an answer to your prayers, so continue seeing and feeling yourself to be at peace.'

Within a matter of weeks, my life was turned upside down and I was riding a very scary rollercoaster of change. There were lots of ups and downs with a few hairy bends thrown in for good measure! The events that followed my weird experience that morning were to take me on a journey of transformation. I became the person I am today, and I will share with you the process of my transformation throughout the pages of this book.

I discovered an almighty truth and power within me that has allowed me to become the creator of my life. And through this, the void has been filled. The something I had been looking and longing for has been finally found. I discovered my place in the world, and it felt like I had come home. I got it. It was like I had been trying to navigate my way through life with a faulty flash torch, only for it to be put on to full beam, allowing me to see the bigger picture. This has been the biggest blessing of my life, and I want to share this blessing with you. This is the reason for me writing this book.

I want to be your full beam and show you that there is an easier way to live your life.

You no longer have to walk alone in the dark. There is a more illuminated path and it's waiting to guide you. So, come take a journey with me, walk with me and let me be your torch.

Throughout the pages of this book, I hope to offer you a new roadmap for your life. I want to give you a fresh perspective, a new authentic purpose and, most importantly, hope for the future.

My aim is to demonstrate that living your life 'on purpose' is actually really easy, and that just a few small baby steps can not only change your world, but the world of those around you.

So turn the page and let's begin our journey.

With love
Your coach

Louise.

Introduction

First things first, put the kettle on!

Go grab yourself a cup of tea. Put your slippers on. Close the door. Switch off your phone and make yourself comfortable.

Now let me be blunt with you for a second. This could be yet another book that you read and then add to your ever-increasing mound of spiritual/self help books, or it can be the book that changes your life. The choice is really yours. This book will be what you want it to be. It just depends on how much you really want change in your life.

Are you ready to put the effort in, to take action and *do things* differently?

If the answer is no, then simply close this book now and carry on with your life as it is. I need you to be totally open and willing before we begin. Otherwise there is no point!

In order to create real change in your life you have to truly want it. You have to be prepared to see things differently, to move beyond your current paradigm and most importantly you have to be willing to get your running shoes on and take action.

This book requires you to do *all three*.

I will stretch your thinking and I will expect you to take action. No action, no change!

There, I said it!

Sometimes as part of my job I have to be super firm and just tell it like it is. We all need this from time-to-time.

So set the intention that this book will be a catalyst for real change and transformation in your life, make a commitment to read, then re-read and to complete all of the assignments set out.

Give yourself fully. Do this and your life will change.

OK, deep breath please, take a sip of your tea… *let's start creating miracles!*

Your 40-Day Miracle Masterplan

Many of us travel through life at breakneck speed. Days roll into months, and months into years and before we know it a decade has passed us by. We peer in the mirror in despair as we detect yet another wrinkle. Time stands still for no man so we must ensure that we make every second count. No one wants to get to 90 and look back with regret wishing they had written that book, opened that seaside café or accepted that wedding proposal. It's painful and leads to bitterness and resentment.

The only way to make sure that you don't end up with a face full of wrinkles and a heart bursting with regret, is to regularly take stock of your life and check-in with yourself. My aim with this book is to help you do just that. Not only will I help you to see your life with fresh eyes, I will provide you with a toolbox of ticks, ideas, strategies and practices that you can use for the rest of your life.

This is a 40-day miracle masterplan, so while you can randomly dip in and out, it will be more powerful if you follow the 40-day plan in order, this way everything will all fit together perfectly and make sense.

Each week we will be focusing on a different topic and at the end of each day there will be a short assignment for you to complete. The assignments are the most important part and will help you embed your learning and take the necessary steps to improve your life.

Here's the rundown:

Week 1 - Get ready to uncover your personal blueprint. If you've ever wondered if you have a life purpose, a reason for being on this planet, week 1 will give you all the answers you've been searching for. You're going to discover your core values, your God-given gifts; you're going to get clear on the environments you best thrive in. You're even going to redefine your definition of success and happiness. Plus I'll be showing you how to show up for your life assignment by tapping into your Inner Guide. It's going to be an enlightening first week!

Week 2 - This is your opportunity to stop the clock, a chance to catch your breath and really take stock of what's working in your life and what's not. I'm going to create an opening for you to bring to the surface your deepest desires and wishes for your future. I'll be sharing my personal road map for success and how to achieve even the biggest of goals. I will also invite you to join my Sunday Night Club!

Week 3 - In week 3 you're taking a journey into the dark crevasse of your mind. I'm going to introduce you to the most powerful forces in your life, your Inner Guide and Inner Critic. You're going to shine a light on all those limiting beliefs that are sabotaging your life and I'll be showing you my secret weapons for rewiring your mind for miracles. It can be done and I'm going to show you exactly how!

Week 4 - I'm going to be revealing powerful practices that have changed my life and have the potential to change yours too. I'll show you how to create an energy vortex in your home, how to tune into your Inner Guide, how to start co-creating with the Universe and, most importantly, how to create a daily practice that will serve you for the rest of your life.

Week 5 - We're talking energy, chakras, meridians, subtle vibrations and finding your energetic flow. I'll be teaching you some basic energy exercises to enhance your life. When energy flows, so do miracles!

Week 6 - Our final week together is all about self-love, self-nurturing and boundaries. It's time to stand in your own power and find your inner goddess! I'll be sharing my most powerful confidence boosting exercises, plus you'll be creating your own personal self-care manifesto and gratitude journal.

Talking My Language

You will notice throughout the book that I use words like *'Divine Infinite Intelligence'*, *'Universe'* *'Inner Guide'* and *'Inner Critic'*. I'd like to take a moment to give you an understanding of what I mean by each phrase.

<u>*'Divine Infinite Intelligence'*</u> could be described as the creator and ruler of the Universe and source of all; the Supreme Being. You may like to think of this as God or the Universe. For me, it's a

powerful entity, an intelligence that goes way beyond the mind. The Divine Infinite Intelligence is of the highest vibration of pure love and makes all life possible on Planet Earth and beyond.

'Inner Guide' I believe we all have an unearthly internal guidance system within us; a bit like a GPS, some call it intuition, higher self, a funny feeling, a hunch, mother's intuition, a feeling in one's bones or simply a gut feeling. Personally I like to think of it as a guardian angel. I believe we all have angels guiding us throughout our life. For the purpose of this book, I will be referring to this guidance as your Inner Guide.

'Inner Critic' this is your negative programming, limiting beliefs and thoughts. Very often your Inner Critic is referred to as your ego. It's the part of the mind that mediates between the conscious and the unconscious and is responsible for reality testing and a sense of personal identity. When I talk about the Inner Critic throughout the book, I mean the negative voice inside your head that constantly tells you're not good enough or that you don't deserve to live an abundant life. In short, it's the voice that holds you back in life.

Ready, Set... Go!

Three final things for you to consider before we begin our journey.

1) Clear your space
I believe that when you're about to take a journey of transformation you need to clear your physical space and make room in your life.

If you're constantly looking at unfinished DIY, unfiled paperwork or cluttered cupboards, it's going to distract you and take your attention away from your work with this book. So before you begin take a couple of days or even hours to literally clear your space, clean your house, sort out your wardrobe, declutter your kitchen cupboards, cut the grass, fix the broken loo seat and clear the old receipts from your purse. Clear the decks, create the space and make room in your life for what is about to come.

2) Go shopping

I suggest you treat yourself to a journal, preferably a beautiful one that you will enjoy writing in. You will use your journal to complete all the assignments throughout this book. Scraps of paper here and there will not do!

3) Recruit help

And finally, you also might like to consider taking this journey with someone else; a friend, a family member or a colleague at work. Support and accountability can make the world of difference. Those who have support and encouragement from those around them achieve amazing feats. Who might you like to recruit on this 40-day Miracle Masterplan?

Ok, we're all set and ready to go… your 40-day Miracle Masterplan starts as soon as you turn the next page…

WEEK 1

DAYS 1-7

Mastering Your Blueprint

PART 1

WEEK 4

DAYS 1–7

Mastering Your
Blueprint

Days 1-7

Mastering Your Blueprint

In the workshops, retreats and courses that I run, I talk a lot about *personal blueprints*. This is also something that I discuss with my private clients, and I touched on it in my first book, *'Finding a Future That Fits'*.

I am *passionate* about teaching people how to uncover their blueprint and recognise what makes them tick, because once we understand this we can consciously start to build our life around what's important to us. We can transform it by living *'on purpose'*.

It really is that simple!

Your blueprint is who you really are underneath all the layers of shoulds and should nots. It's your essence, your core and the person you came to this planet to be.

Yet we are born into this crazy world of false ideals; we live by the rules of society and before too long we forget who we are and how to bring our spirit alive. You are only *truly* alive when your spirit can come out and play. All too often, we look outside of ourselves to define who we are. We see our contemporaries achieving success and believe that we must strive for the same things. We feel the pressure to study a particular subject, get on the housing ladder and start a family before it's too late. We believe that we will find meaning and purpose in the material things that we are taught to covet. Before long we've created a noose around our neck. We wind up looking at our life, feeling totally adrift and disorientated and thinking, *"How the hell did I get here?"*

I believe that we're too focused on what's going on *'out there'*. We've forgotten that the true fulfillment we seek lies *inside us*. To sum up, we're looking for our happiness in all the wrong places. It's like the blind leading the blind and we end up living a life that doesn't feel authentic to who we are.

Your blueprint is the *fundamental bedrock of who you are*. You came here to live your blueprint; to be yourself is your purpose in life. But you can't be yourself if you're living to someone else's ideal.

When your spiritual compass is broken, you will never find a future that truly fits. You will never feel like you've arrived. The only way I can describe living your blueprint is that it's like going home.

The *Divine Infinite Intelligence* simply wants to express itself through you. This can only happen if you are living your unique blueprint. Think of an oak tree. It is programmed by nature to develop and grow from a small delicate acorn into something large and formidable. The oak tree is in *total* unison with nature; it grows with the flow of nature and doesn't decide one day that it would rather be a weeping willow! Nor does it look to other trees and think that it should be more like them. It stands proud in its own power knowing what and who it is. It's aware that in order to be the fullest and most magnificent version of itself, it must be itself and let nature lead the way.

Sadly, we've forgotten how to ride in the universal flow of nature like all other plants and animals do. You are born to be you and only you. You are not your job, you are not just someone's daughter, wife and mother, and you are not defined by how much money you have in the bank, how many qualifications you possess, or the type of house you live in. You are perfect and whole and more than enough just as you are. Created by the Divine, you are on this planet to be yourself and nobody does you better. This is your purpose.

In my early 20s, my life was pretty much defined by how much money I earned, what job I had, the car I drove, the clothes I wore and the holidays I went on. I was very much wrapped up in the material world. I wasn't unhappy with life, but it lacked meaning and purpose. And deep inside, I knew this. I felt the call within urging me to dig deeper, but fear and ignorance held me back and kept me trapped. When I did finally wake up I started to peel back the layers of Louise and explore who I was beyond all my material possessions. I uncovered what I was passionate about, what my values were and why it was so important to start building my life around them. I got very clear on my God-given gifts, and I started to realise that there was a supreme guiding force waiting for me to wake up so it could assist me in becoming the person that I came to this planet to be.

Until you are willing to wake up and get to the point in life when you think, *"there has to be more to life than this,"* you are a slave to your ego and will miss the miracles that life has in store for you.

I believe that the younger generation of today is much more spiritually conscious. It doesn't take much to awaken them to their truth and internal power. And this powerful high vibrational generation is the one that will transform our world. I truly believe this.

Emma, one of my clients, came to me a few years back feeling very unhappy. She was just about to turn 30 and was feeling very depressed about where she was in her life. She was high up in a large IT corporation and despite earning a substantial income with an impressive status, she was intensely miserable. Each day she would work for 12 hours and then come home to her large, empty flat in Central London. Despite her achievements and success, she was lonely and unfulfilled. She told me that she had always imagined that she would be married and living in the country with a few kids around her ankles by the time she hit 30. Her life wasn't panning out how she expected, but fortunately she was prepared and ready to re-evaluate things before it was too late. Together we worked on defining her blueprint, her core life values, her passions and interests, her gifts and her likes and dislikes. Slowly she started to build a picture of who she really was and what she really wanted. She literally redefined her definition of success. As a result, the next 18 months turned out to be the most exciting and transformational of Emma's life. Within this time she retrained to become a primary school teacher, quit her job in the city and moved to the country to pursue her new life. She took up her childhood passion of horse riding again, and started taking better care of herself. She literally transformed into a new woman.

Becoming totally clear on her blueprint enabled her to consciously navigate her life in the direction that she wanted to go in, and, most importantly, in one that would feed her soul and spirit.

In this very first week of my 40-day programme, I will be sharing with you how to uncover your *own personal blueprint*. Think of it as building a jigsaw puzzle. Each day we will uncover a new piece of the puzzle until we can see the full picture of who you are.

Here's a brief rundown of what I'll be getting you to do this week:

Day 1

This is about getting clear on your core life values and seeing what makes you tick. You'll need to dig deep and examine whether your current life reflects your values right now.

Day 2

We will uncover your superpowers - your God-given gifts - before showing you how you can start using them to reshape your future.

Day 3

We will discover what lights your fire, what brings your spirit alive and makes you want to jump out of bed. And most importantly, we'll discuss how to bring more passion and drive into your life.

Day 4

We will look at the environments that best support you - where you feel most comfortable and at peace - and how you can spend more time in these places.

Day 5

We will redefine your definition of success, and get you to really start thinking about your own unique life direction and what you truly want to see in your future.

Day 6

This is all about finding your purpose in life and discovering what you came to this planet to do.

Day 7

Your time for reflection and rest.

Day 1 – Finding Your V Spot

One of the most important things I discovered in my journey to understanding my own personal blueprint was my core life values. This vital information changed my entire direction in life. It was the first time that I had taken a look inside myself to discover my motivators and drivers. It gave me a much deeper understanding of who I was, and it helped me to navigate my future in a much more positive and purposeful direction. This awareness continues to serve me each and every day of my life.

Your core life values are the fundamental bedrock of who you are as a human being. And everyone's are different. Some people want to feel peace, love and security, while others want recognition, passion and constant challenge. We all have different drivers in life. We are all longing to feel a certain way, whether we are aware of this or not. When we are totally clear about our core life values we can consciously start moving towards getting them met in a healthy and positive way.

When I first worked out what my core life values were, I realised that my *'freedom'* value was vitally important to me. When someone or something impinges on my sense of freedom, I'm not a happy bunny. I had never realised this before, but when I stood back I could see that I've always needed to feel a certain amount of liberation. I love nothing better than a lazy Sunday with nothing to do, I love making my own decisions in life, running my own business and walking in nature. When I'm feeling free I'm content, at peace and at my happiest!

Interestingly, when I looked back at all the jobs I'd ever had, it became very apparent to me that the ones I'd hated and stayed at for the least amount of time were the ones where I'd had the least amount of freedom, i.e., my boss was controlling or I was micro-managed. The jobs I had stayed the longest in were the ones where I'd had the most amount of freedom and was left to work as I pleased. This was so enlightening for me as I quickly realised that I would never truly be happy working for someone else. As a result, I made a conscious decision to start working towards a career that would offer me more independence.

So ask yourself:

1) How do you want to *feel each day* when you drive to work?
2) When you pick up your groceries?
3) When you look at your 'to do' list for the week?
4) When you walk into your office?
5) When you answer your phone?
6) When you pick up your kids from school?
7) When you get dressed in the morning?
8) When you finish your assignment?
9) When you take on that new client?

Getting their core life values met is the single most important gift that a person can give to themselves in a lifetime. Yet many of us our totally blind to what they actually are. We set New Year's resolutions and goals, we strategise and plan, but what we don't see is that the things we're working towards are totally out of alignment with who we are and how we really want to feel.

We think that when we've got that book deal, or the dream job, or the 100k in the bank, or the husband, or the baby, everything will be okay. Yet when we get there, it doesn't feel anything like we thought it would. We've all experienced this. Yes?

All of the things we want on the outside are being driven by a desire to feel a certain way on the inside. It's so important to put our energy into working towards the things that are in alignment with our soul and our core life values, or we will end up filling our lives with meaningless, unfulfilling goals that make us feel flat and empty. We have it totally back-to-front. Before we set our life goals, we must get clear on who we really are and how we really want to feel. You want to work towards things that are going to light up your life, things that feed your soul and give you a deep sense of peace and contentment.

It's time to be honest with yourself. When you get very clear about how you want to feel in life, you gain much better clarity about what goals are the right ones for you.

Uncovering core life values is one of the key exercises I work through with my private clients. I recall one conversation that I had with a lovely client who discovered that one of her values was to feel inspired. When I enquired how often she felt this she thought for a few seconds and told me that she couldn't remember the last time she felt alive and inspired by anything. Then I asked her to think back to a time when inspiration was flowing. Again, she thought long and hard and told me that she used to love to make stuff: crafts, cards, paintings, and so on. She told me that when she was younger she was always learning something new and attending classes and courses, but life had got busy and there simply wasn't the time. I asked her to make a list with me of all the things she'd like to do if there were no limitations on her, such as time. As soon as she gave herself permission to explore this possibility, the ideas started flooding through. All of a sudden she was feeling more inspired than she had done in years, and that was just by brainstorming ideas, let alone actually doing them. This was a huge turning point for her as she realised that she'd neglected this part of herself and wasn't getting her values met.

Another client of mine highlighted that one of her core life values was simply to feel special. But I could tell that revealing this truth about herself was making her feel uncomfortable. Upon enquiring, she told me that surely it was bad to want to feel special, surely that was egoistical. She felt guilty and ashamed for wanting to feel this way. I pointed out that unless she allowed herself to feel special and shine her light, she was holding herself back from living life to the full. I asked her what would be different in her life if she allowed herself to feel special. She replied that that she would start her business, write her book and share it with the world. Getting our core life values met lights us up and makes us shine more brightly than ever before.

The truth is, when you get your core life values met,
you are in total alignment with the Divine,
you are in the flow of life, and when you're in the flow
you attract miracles into your path.

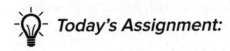 *Today's Assignment:*

How do you want to feel in your life?

Today, I simply want you to take 20 minutes for yourself to brainstorm all of the ways you'd like to feel in life. Here are a few feeling words to get you going: free, excited, affectionate, challenged, powerful, important, special, harmonious, peaceful, loving, playful, connected, protected, driven. Ask your subconscious to bring up all the ways you love to feel.

It can be very useful to think about past events in your life that you've really enjoyed and ask yourself, *"How was I feeling in that moment?"* This will help bring to your attention your core life values.

Write down as many as you can think of, and then start amalgamating or eliminating those ones that don't feel right. Tune into your intuition here... you know! You're aiming for about *six core life values*. Write them on Post-it notes and stick them to a wall in your house. Sleep on it. Leave them there for a couple of days or so and see how you feel about them then. Would you still pick the same ones? Would you add more? Is there something missing?

Now list *10 experiences* or *accomplishments* that will get your core life values met more often. What's the one thing that you can do today to get at least one of your values met?

The most important thing you can do once you have defined your core life values is to start building your life around them, and use them as a life compass. Make decisions and set goals and intentions that are in total alignment with your core life values. *Do this and your life will transform before your eyes.*

Day 2 – Discover Your Superpowers

Part of uncovering your blueprint involves becoming clear on what I call your *superpowers*, or *God-given gifts*.

I believe that we are all here with a *Divine Purpose in life*. We are all on this planet to make our mark in some way, and to use our talents, skills, passions and gifts. Yet most of us play a small part, not really recognising the untapped potential that we have within us.

Whether you're ready to hear this or not, I'm here to tell you that you are on this planet with a special mission and your job is to simply use your gift in some way to help others. And the great thing is, using your God-given gifts will always be in alignment with your core life values - always! Using your superpowers feels magical and very natural. But the sad thing is, most people can't *see* their superpowers. Your God-given gifts are so much part of who you are that they are almost invisible to you. It's like trying to see the end of your nose.

There are those people who have natural talents for making people laugh, for healing, or for nature. There are those who have natural talents for creating inspiring works of art, for playing a musical instrument, or singing in perfect tune. There are those who can sell ice to Eskimos, or are awesome at finding a bargain in a charity shop. We all have something we're awesome at, whether we're aware of it or not.

It's this differentiation that makes this world such a diverse place to live. I believe that each one of us shares the common purpose of contributing something of value to this world using our unique set of passions, values and talents. The answer to discovering your God-given gifts lies inside you right now.

Interestingly, when we are children, we instinctively know what we enjoy doing, what comes naturally and what we're good at. Whether that's building sandcastles or Lego, drawing pictures or baking fairy cakes. As children, we simply follow our hearts and do what we naturally find most enjoyable and fun.

Unfortunately, as we get older, we lose touch with these natural abilities. Our God-given gifts tend to get covered up quite early on in life and many of us lose touch with them by the time we reach adulthood. We literally forget who we are. Our parents, teachers or friends might say, *"You'll never be able to do that"*, *"You're just not clever enough,"* or *"You can't do that, be more realistic"*, and we accept these as the limitations of our world and wind up travelling down paths that we were never meant to go down. When our lives are in conflict with our natural God-given gifts, we feel disappointed, tired, burdened, frustrated and let down by life.

For example, I could easily have become a maths teacher (at a very basic level), but maths was not a subject I enjoyed, nor was I particularly good at it, so to build a career around it would have been futile. Instead, I decided to create a career I truly enjoyed which encompassed all of my natural talents and abilities. The result is that I love what I do and wake up each morning with a spring in my step and passion for the day ahead.

Here's the crux of my message today:

'Our God-given gifts really are the fundamental core of who we are, and when we can learn to build our lives around them we will become much more fulfilled and satisfied.'

One thing I know for sure is this:

'You are on this planet for a special reason and that involves using your superpowers!'

If you want to uncover your God-given gifts and ultimately your life's calling, a good place to start is your childhood. Remember who you were when you were dancing around the living room performing for your aunties and uncles, or when you came in at the end of the day with mud up to your armpits after looking for creepy crawlies. I want to encourage you to bring those feelings back and remember your childhood as best you can. I appreciate that it may seem like many moons ago, so dig out some old photos to provoke some memories, or talk to your family about their recollections. This will help you rediscover what you left behind.

If you can't remember the exact things that you liked doing, just substitute it. What was it that you enjoyed most about performing in front of your aunties and uncles or getting your hands dirty? Was it being the centre of attention or the excitement of discovery?

I watch my children with enthusiasm, because I want to encourage them to develop their God-given gifts and continue to use them in their adult lives. This way, they will feel connected to who they really are and their life purpose will become clear to them as they develop and grow. They will never feel lost if they stay connected to who they really are.

My son has an innate gift for riding his bicycle. Most kids can do this, of course, but his ability is way beyond the norm. In fact, his gross motor skills have always been super developed, even from a young age. He walked at 11 months, started running at 12 months, and he could balance on a climbing frame by 14 months. He was so coordinated and fast at everything he did that people were always commenting. Needless to say, starting school was a challenge for him as he is far better suited to being outside than cooped up in a classroom. At 18 months we put him on his first balance bike and he was off. It was at this point we realised that he has a real talent for riding. At every opportunity he was outside on this bike. His bike literally goes everywhere with us: to school, to nanny's house, even to Sainsbury's!

By the age of 4, my son was competing and winning all his races at the National Strider Championships that we took him to. Who knows where it'll lead, but as long as he's enjoying himself we will continue to allow him to develop his gift.

My daughter, on the other hand, loves to write stories and draw. I'm always finding stories on the most creative of subjects floating around the house. Her creativity and imagination is just wonderful. I'm determined to encourage her to develop her talent and passion.

It's time to see what's hidden at the end of your nose. *What are your God-given gifts?*

Like everyone on the planet, you too have God-given gifts. And when you uncover them and start using them your life will flourish in unimaginable ways. Remember, using your gifts is your purpose and your core mission on this planet. Start using them as much as you can, develop them and share them with those around you. Allow yourself to open up to the possibility that you can make your mark on this planet by using your gifts. This is your purpose in life.

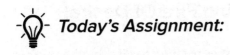 *Today's Assignment:*

Here are six *very important* questions to get you thinking about your God-given gifts:

1) What do you find comes easy to you?
2) When growing up, what were you gifted at or had a talent for?
3) What makes you excited and animated, or lights up your face?
4) What activities make you lose all sense of time?
5) What are you drawn to doing?
6) If you were to ask your family or friends what your natural talents are, what would they say? If you're not sure about this one, ask them directly!

Day 3 – Your Burning Fire Of Desire!

It's day three folks, and today we're going to take another look at a piece of the jigsaw puzzle. Today we're talking passion!

Now, before we begin with today's assignment, let me share with you the definition of passion:

'Passion is when you put more energy into something than is required. It is more than just enthusiasm or excitement, passion is ambition that is materialised into action to put as much heart, mind, body and soul into something as is possible.'

Just like core life values and our God-given gifts, we all have things that ignite us and make us come alive. When we are passionate about something our vibes are naturally high and it's like a light has been switched on inside of us. We are at our most vibrant and animated.

There are people who are passionate about human rights, ecology, spirituality, food, children, art, history, travel, design, sports, fashion, community, people, education, politics. The list is endless! And it makes total sense to put our energy towards things that we're passionate about, whether that is professionally or personally.

How do you know what you're passionate about? Well, you naturally gravitate towards a subject, activity or hobby that you are passionate about. When you overhear a conversation on something you're passionate about, you naturally want to join in. When you're passionate about something you can't wait to get up in the morning and get on with it. Your passion almost becomes the driving force in your life. It can almost become all-consuming! Some people have many passions, some people have just a few, some people move from one passion to the next and some people are yet to discover their passions.

My husband doesn't like the word passion. He prefers to think of it as *'interests'*. During the 16 years we've been together, he's had many interests, from biking and running to writing music and doing DIY, all of which he's thrown himself into fully. But one thing I know for sure is this: when he puts his energy into an activity or project he becomes *totally* passionate about it!

Personally, I'm passionate about education, teaching and spiritually. I'm constantly reading educational books, and I'm always teaching and sharing ideas and new concepts. I'm also very passionate about ecology and natural living. All of these subjects naturally bring me alive.

Some of my private clients struggle to find their passion; they tell me that they have interests but nothing that really gets them super excited. Some people just haven't found their passion yet. They haven't given themselves the space to really explore and find out what makes them come alive. It's like they've almost resigned themselves to the fact that this is as good as life's going to get, so they stop looking! But remember, we're here to play the *game of life*.

> *If you're unclear about what your passions are,*
> *it's time to start exploring!*

I lived the first 25 years of my life totally unaware and in the dark. I hadn't got a clue what my core life values were, and I certainly didn't think I had any God-given gifts. The only thing I thought I was passionate about was shoes! As a result, I was only living a half-life (with a very large wardrobe). I felt like there was a constant void in my life and I found myself looking to fill it in all the wrong places. No matter how vast my wardrobe, it was never going to fulfill me in the way living my purpose would. It wasn't until I opened up to the possibility that there had to be more to life, that there must be something I was missing, that hey presto, the Divine heard my call and started to deliver the vital missing pieces of the jigsaw that had been absent from my life. I slowly started to piece things together.

When you're passionate, you naturally want to spend as much time indulging in your passion as you can. You can't help yourself. You want to share your ideas with your friends and family, you yearn to talk to other like-minded people and share your passion with them. But here's something important that I want you to hear. You can earn a living from your passion. In fact, your mission in life is to earn a living from your passions. Yep, you heard me. Gone are the days when you had to spend your entire career doing unfulfilling, boring and soul-destroying work.

Let me remind you, you are here to live your core life values, to use your gifts and to have as much passion as you can stand.

How good are you willing to let your life get? It's time to play, to explore and to discover what lights your fire!

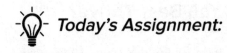 *Today's Assignment:*

Take 20 minutes alone and answer the following questions:

1) What subjects do you adore and love to be involved in?
2) What things are you naturally drawn to?
3) When do you lose all sense of time?
4) What do you love to chat about most with friends over a glass of red?
5) What magazine or books do you love to read?
6) What conference or event would you like to attend this year and what is it about?
7) What kind of advice do you enjoy giving to people?
8) What do people come to you for?
9) If you were someone's 'phone a friend', what subjects would they phone you about?
10) What do you want to be known for?
11) What things/activities would you like to explore in order to find your passion?

Day 4 – Where Do You Best Thrive?

When we surround ourselves in happy, healthy and inspiring surroundings, there is no doubt that it lifts our spirits and feeds our soul. When we're in a supportive environment, we are connected and therefore have better clarity. We get better ideas, and feel more energised and alive. When we spend time in heavy, toxic and negative surroundings, we tend to feel sluggish, anxious and uninspired. This can have a detrimental effect on us emotionally, spiritually and physically.

Think about how you feel when you take a walk in nature, visit your favourite shop, potter around your home or garden, swim in the sea, attend a live gig, go to a dance or yoga class and travel about on the bus, train or in the car. Notice the effect different environments have on the way you feel from day to day.

Everything is energy. It is a mass of millions of vibrating molecules and atoms. From people, nature, our homes and place of work, to inanimate objects such as the chair you're sitting in right now. Everything holds a particular vibration that we can feel with our sixth sense. Whether you've ever really thought about this or not, we intuitively know this to be true, and at some level we pick up and absorb the vibrations all around us. We've all experienced walking into a room and feeling a harsh, negative force looming in the air. Conversely, when we walk into a big arena before a concert, we can literally feel the excitement in the air - it's electric! Our bodies are astonishingly good at sensing how a particular environment feels to us. It's like having an antenna to help us determine whether an environment is good for us or not.

We all have favourite environments in which we prefer to spend time. And it's important for us to become aware of where we are at our happiest. It naturally makes sense for us to spend as much time in environments that support us as possible.

As a sensitive soul myself, I found working in a corporate environment really difficult to deal with. By the end of a day filled with meeting, clients, and workplace gossip I'd find myself feeling flat and listless. Have you ever experienced this? I have always struggled with environments such as shopping malls, open plan offices and busy city centres, where there are large groups of people. I always come away from them feeling exhausted.

I love to spend time at home. My home is my sanctuary and it nourishes me. I feel safe, secure and connected in my home environment. But our homes hold many energies and aren't always places of peace and tranquility. People, clutter or unfinished DIY can really affect the energy of a home.

The truth is, many of us spend too much time in harmful environments that deplete our life force energy. These environments disconnect us from the Divine and it's vital that we become aware of the ones that really support us and lift us up. The more time we spend in healthy environments, the happier and more connected we will be.

So, today I want to get you thinking about your own personal surroundings, both at work and at home.

Think about environments where you feel inspired and motivated. Then consider the places where you feel the most relaxed and peaceful. Which areas are fun and exhilarating? Where do you feel most connected to your inner power? Now think about how can you spend more time in these favourite environments.

If you are happiest at home but spend all week in an office at your workplace, it's vitally important that you give yourself plenty of downtime at home come the weekend. If you find your work environment particularly toxic, just taking a short walk at lunchtime can make a massive difference.

If your home is full of housemates, children or family, you might find that taking a walk around the block is the time when you feel most connected. Some of my clients say that just sitting in their car alone gives them the peace they need. I remember spending many of my lunchtimes in my car reading, meditating or listening to music. It did me the world of good just to escape the workplace for a while.

Kate, one of my clients, thrives best when she's outside with her horses; being indoors too long drives her crazy and lowers her mood. She gets all her best ideas while outside.

Fran, another client, loves the sea. She told me that she finds something magical about walking on the beach and listening to the waves lap back and forth. But Fran pointed out that she lived 150 miles inland and visiting the seaside wasn't something she was able to do often. Together we explored how she could generate that same feeling without having to do a 300 mile round trip. She decided that she would take regular baths and buy a CD with nature/seaside sounds. When we met for her next session she told me what a difference it was making. Every few nights she would lock herself away in the bathroom, light a few candles, lay in the bath, play her CD and visualise sitting by the water's edge. She told me that she was able to totally lose herself in the moment and it felt awesome.

Sometimes we need to think outside the box and remember that our mind can literally take us anywhere in the world!

Choosing the right environment might sound very simple, but in order to really find ourselves we have to ensure that our surroundings support and nurture us. When we do this, we are more able to connect with our intuition, and when we are connected, we get all the life guidance we could ever need or want. Our aim in life is to stay balanced and connected to the Divine as much as possible, and our environment plays a huge part in this.

 Today's Assignment:

Take a few moments to answer the following questions:
1) What are your top three favourite environments?
2) Why do you love them so much?
3) How do they make you feel?
4) How can you spend more time in environments that nourish and support you?
5) How can you make your current environment more supportive?

Day 5 – Redefining Success?

Sometimes we get swept up in comparisons (aka *compare and despair*). We look in from the outside at other people's lives and we think… she's thinner than me, she has longer hair than me, she has more sex than me or she earns way more than me.

Ever found yourself doing this?

In the age of social media, we have 24-7 access to everyone else's *'highlights reel'*. We get to see our friends' latest holiday photos to sunny Barbados, their new über cool state-of-the-art kitchen, their latest designer shoes and even what they've had for their bloody dinner!

It's so easy to compare ourselves and then feel bad about where we are based on what we see others doing. It's exhausting, discouraging and moreover, if we're not careful, it makes us feel *totally inadequate*. It's a losing game whichever way you look at it.

As a businesswoman and mum-of-two, I also find myself falling into the compare and despair trap. Yes, I am human! I often find myself eyeing up someone's shiny new car, or comparing my work to my competitors. We all get caught up to a certain extent. But what I've come to notice is this: the more I compare myself to others, whether that is in business or in my personal life, the more I lose touch with my true, authentic self.

I find myself veering off course trying to be someone I'm not,
or trying to attain something that I don't even want!

As I write, I'm taken back to a recent event where I almost derailed from my own happiness and success plan. I found myself looking at what other business owners were achieving, and how they were earning their money and running their businesses. And I found myself questioning myself. Was their way better than mine? Maybe I'd got it all wrong and should follow their model. Now, I knew in my heart that what they were doing didn't feel right to me, but I gave my power away as I started to doubt myself. I had allowed myself to get lost in the outer world and was ignoring my inner world and personal truth. Thankfully, my questioning was only fleeting. I quickly woke up and remembered my mission and my own definition of success and happiness. I was soon off on my merry way again. Crazy when you think about it. But the truth is, I'm a pretty self-aware kind of gal. I know who I am and I know what I stand for, yet I can still find myself getting caught up with thinking the grass is greener on the other side.

The more we *compare* our lives to others, the more we lose touch with ourselves, our core life values, our God-given gifts, our passions and ultimately, our mission in life. And in all honesty, no one lives a truly perfect life. Is there such a thing? We all have our trials and tribulations and it's about making the most of what we have and enjoying our life to the full. There will always be more to achieve and more to buy. Will we ever arrive at perfect peace, with everything just as we want, every box ticked and every ambition or goal met? Probably not.

Next week, we are going to turn our focus towards what our goals and intentions are. Before we do this, it's vitally important that you get totally clear on what success and happiness looks like for you. Do this without comparing yourself to other people's idea of success. It's such a personal thing, yet very few of us ever give this any thought. We follow the flock, doing what others do, wanting what others have, and we don't tune into our own desires. We see that our friend has just been promoted and had a raise, and this makes us feel unsettled. We start imagining that we too must strive for the same without really thinking about whether a promotion is right for us or not. We see our best friend get married and we feel pressure to do the same. But is this really what you want? Is now the right time for you? We really need to stop looking outside of ourselves to define who we really are and what we really want from life.

Ask yourself this: *"What is my definition of success and happiness? What do I really want from my life?"*

A good way to do this is to imagine that you're 90-years-old and looking back at your life. It has been happy, rich and fulfilling with no regrets whatsoever. What do you see? What things did you achieve? Where did you live? Who did you share your life with?

It's OK to want material things: a BMW, lots of holiday, a walk-in wardrobe, or a new sofa for your living room. It's not unspiritual to be financially abundant. The Divine wants us to be happy and provided for. But it's also important to think about what you want your legacy to be. If you are to leave the world a better place, how will you have contributed?

My definition of success and happiness is quite simple, and here's my list:

- ★ Living my life connected to spirit.
- ★ Freedom to run my own life as I wish.
- ★ Being the best mummy that I can be for my children, and to know in my heart that I did my best.

- ★ Having a secure and happy relationship with my hubby.
- ★ Serving and inspiring others via my work, books, speaking and programmes.
- ★ Being financially free.
- ★ Being able to give back to the developing world in some way.
- ★ Travelling the globe.
- ★ Having a beautiful home in the country.

It's *very important* that you let go of any predetermined ideas about what success should look like. This is not about what your parents think, or your best friend, or your boss, your neighbours, your partner, your kids. What is your definition of success and happiness?

We must remain steadfast to our own definition of success and happiness, and not be lured into someone else's! Your definition of success is really about living your blueprint and getting your core life values met.

 ### *Today's Assignment:*

Write down your own definition of success and happiness in the following areas of your life.

Tune into your own inner guide and ensure that it's your definition and not your parents', siblings', friends', partner's, etc. Remember to also think about how you want to FEEL in each of these areas, not just what you want to achieve materially.

➤ Home
➤ Work or career
➤ Finances
➤ Romantic life
➤ Family life
➤ Friendships
➤ Personal growth
➤ Spiritual or religious
➤ Fun

Pin your list on your wall as a reminder.

Remember, don't live your life by someone else's definition.

When you find yourself veering off course trying to be someone you're not, or trying to attain something that you don't even want, remind yourself what is really important *to you*.

Day 6 – What's Your Life Assignment?

One thing I know for sure is that we are all here with a Divine purpose. We are all on this planet to make our mark in some way, and to use our talents, skills, passions and gifts.

There is a world waiting to be born through you. You have a higher purpose, whether you're able to see this yet or not. Playing small doesn't serve you, and it certainly doesn't serve the world at large. Yet many of us fall into unfulfilling work and believe that this is our lot. We tell ourselves that we should be grateful and put up and shut up. Years pass by and before long a decade has been and gone and all we've gained is a heap of wrinkles. We wind up feeling disheartened and let down by life.

Nothing upsets me more than to see someone wasting their life in a stuffy office working for someone else when they could be out there making a difference and shining their light.

The world needs as many game changers as possible right now. We're in an exciting time of evolution, and we have work to do!

Deep down we feel the call, and know that there is something bigger than us, something more than we can see. And the sad thing is, when we are not on our true Divine path we feel lost, unfulfilled and even resentful as we see others enjoying life and living their highest calling.

Yes we hear the call, yes we feel the tap on the shoulder, but more often than not, we drown it out with another glass of chardonnay, or another gorgeous pair of new shoes. Invariably, this doesn't work. These material things will never, ever fill the void that living your purpose brings.

So how do you *find your calling?* How do you make a difference in the world and get paid well to do it?

Earlier this week we looked at your blueprint, your core life values, your passions, your God-given gifts, your surroundings, and so on. Your blueprint is the fundamental bedrock of who you are. It's what makes you tick, what makes your heart sing and brings you alive. You cannot live a purposeful life if you don't know who you are. Understand who you are and your purpose will become illuminated.

The first thing you must do is change your belief about what is possible and be totally open to the notion that you are here to make a difference in the world. You have a Divine mission, everyone does, so don't allow yourself to play small anymore.

As I ventured on to my spiritual path, and started to really explore who I was, I remember thinking, *"What if I don't have a life purpose? What if living my purpose means I'll have to leave the security of my job?"* and *"What happens if God has big plans for me, but I don't want to do them?"*

But here's the thing that I've come to realise. Your purpose doesn't feel like hard work. Your purpose feels more like play. It makes your heart sing and you want to jump out of bed every day because you love what you do. Your purpose naturally generates your core life values. It puts you in the right surroundings with like-minded people and you naturally use your God-given gifts effortlessly. Living your purpose isn't hard. Yes, you'll have to make a few scary leaps from time to time, but it'll be worth it. So allow yourself to be open to change and be willing to be of service. Trust that there is something more for you.

I went to see Doreen Virtue in London a while back and I remember her saying that we are all employees of the Universe. We all have an assignment to carry out in our lifetime, it's just whether we're brave enough to put our hand up and say, *"I'm ready for my assignment please."* The great thing about being an employee of the Universe is that you cannot be fired and the Divine will pay you kindly.

What I have come to understand is that for each of us, there are many different kinds of assignment. As long as we are using our God-given gifts and we're passionate about it, we will find our assignment fulfilling. I adore being a coach and mentor, it ticks all the boxes for me, but I could quite easily have been a fashion advisor and loved it just as much. It would still be ticking all the right boxes and using my gifts.

Living your purpose is about being the highest possible version of yourself. It's about expressing yourself and being fully you. In truth, your Divine purpose is to bring more of your authentic self to this world.

Some people's purpose is very public and their mission is to teach, enlighten, heal or create on a national or global scale. For others, living their purpose is closer to home and about making a difference within their community or family home. No purpose it more or less important than another.

It's important that we open our eyes. There are many ways that we can live out our purpose, and we're not necessarily looking for just one route.

We have to get brave and ask. When you're willing to be of service, the Divine immediately responds and it starts to get to work to bring everything - and I mean everything - you need to bring you directly to your purpose. The Divine can do all of this for you, but you have to take the action first. Yes, you have to step up to the plate and say, *"I'm going to do this. I'm scared but I'm ready."* When you do this you will notice positive changes happening. You may have a chance meeting with old friends or colleagues, emails will start pinging into your inbox, a letter will come through your door, an inspiring thought will pop into your mind, or you'll see something helpful on TV. The Divine is constantly trying to get our attention and give us the information we need, but are we awake enough to notice?

Remember folks, I've been there. I've gone from living in the void of despair to finding and living my purpose each and every day. There have been lots of highs and lows, but I've come to learn that inspired people, who are living their life on purpose, inspire others. The natural tendency of a motivated, wide-awake individual is to awaken and enthuse others. As you shine your light, you allow others to shine theirs. It's that simple.

Now imagine the transformed world that we'd all be benefiting from if we were all living on purpose and using our God-given gifts.

I'm not going to tell you it'll be easy, but I am here to tell you it'll be worth it. Knowing that you are living your purpose each and every day is the biggest blessing you can have.

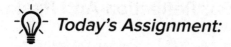 *Today's Assignment:*

We are going to pull all of the information you've gathered about yourself this week together in *one place*.

You're going to create your *blueprint* on a large piece of paper. (How you do this is up to you.) You can create columns if you wish, or you can sketch out a flower and write in each petal. Your objective is to list your core life values, your passions and interests, your God-given gifts, your favourite environments, your definition of success, and anything else that you feel is necessary.

Then I'd like you to do a brain dump of all the possibilities open to you. There are infinite opportunities available, whether you are able to see this yet or not. Remember, we are employees of the Universe. We just have to put our hand up and ask, *"What's my assignment?"* Then the Divine will lead you in that direction.

I want you to imagine that you're 90 and looking back at your wonderful life. What do you see? What would you like your legacy to be? Is it about becoming a mother? Writing a book? Teaching? Healing work? Creating? Working within your community? Starting a business? Working abroad? Travelling the world? Doing charity work? Don't leave anything out.

Ask yourself this question: *"How can I make my mark on the world?"*

Create a brain dump on a large piece of paper, or buy a little ideas book that you can carry about with you.

Keep asking the question and you <u>will</u> get your answer!

Day 7 – Your Day For Reflection And Rest

Take time today to let what you have learned this week sink in.

Also, take a couple of minutes to answer the following questions:

1) What insights have you gained about yourself this week?
2) What have you discovered about yourself that you weren't aware of before?
3) How are you feeling about what you have learned?
4) How might this change your life for the better?
5) What is the most important thing that you must now do?

Prayer for this week:

"Dear Divine Guidance, thank you for helping me to strip back the layers that no longer serve me and are stopping the real me from shining forth. Please guide me in a direction that makes my heart sing, clearly showing me who I am and what I came to this planet to do. Show me how to live my purpose so I might inspire others to do the same."

And so it is.

WEEK 2

DAYS 8-14

Mastering Your Big Vision

Days 8-14

Mastering Your Big Vision

Now that you have spent some time digging a little deeper into the true essence of who you *really* are, it's time to decide what you want from the rest of your life. You can't determine what you want from life until you know who you are. That's a fact.

This second week is all about taking stock of what's not working in your life and then deciding on which direction you want to travel in. We're going to reset your compass and set you off on a brand new path. Exciting, eh?

You're going to be using what you've learned in week one to assist you in setting some big, life-changing goals. Week two is about bringing the *spiritual* and the *practical* together. I believe that this is what I'm on this planet to teach, because when you bring the spiritual and the practical to the party, it's going to be a celebration that you'll never forgot.

I'm going to be showing you firstly how to take stock of where you're at in your life - what is and isn't serving you. From here, you can really hone in on the areas of your life that need your attention, whether that's your job, your love life, your health, your finances, and so on. I'm going to be encouraging you to set big goals that are really going to push you out of your comfort zone - in a good way. We're not talking wishy-washy goals here, we're talking about the *rock-your-world* kind of goals!

When I realised that we can have whatever we want in life, that we are co-creators and not victims, as I previously thought, I started to up my game and ask for what I really wanted. It's not enough to want to lose a few pounds, or pay off that darned credit card, or take a week's holiday to Ibiza. This isn't really stretching yourself, is it?! You will never live your purpose in life without *dreaming big*. Vague desires and unformed longing will never cut the mustard. It's not enough; the Divine wants more from you.

> *You've got to play big in this world, and you've got to get super clear. Don't keep yourself small.*

You were never born to be small; you were born to play your part in the miracle of life, to explore, to expand, to grow and to live life to the absolute max. *This is your Divine calling.*

The more clear and focused you are about what you want, the more you create the mental image in your mind's eye. The more you take action in the right direction, the stronger your desires will be and the quicker you'll manifest them into your life. And when your desire is strong, when you are steadfast to your big vision, it will be yours. The Divine will deliver - that's a promise.

So first and foremost this week, we are going to get clear on your goals and what you *really want* from your life. After that we'll turn our attention to the '*a*' word - *action*.

For now I'd like to give you a little insight into how I work with my private clients. When I decide to work with a brand new client, my first job is to get clear on their intentions and goals. It's then about creating a plan of action to ensure that we reach that goal. We take consistent action to make sure we're moving closer and closer to the desired outcome. This is coaching in its basic form. When people have this kind of support and accountability, they can move mountains, they really can! Having accountability, focus and support is like having a friend cheering you on, and this makes an immense difference to how quickly you can reach your goals.

One of the key areas where people go wrong is that although they may have the most amazing ideas and gifts to share, they never do anything about them. They never actually take real action. This pains me greatly because I see so much potential that is wasted because of lack of action. Action is the engine to your dreams. *Without action, nothing changes.* I know that taking action can sometimes be scary, but fear is part of the human growth process. If you want to change your life, you've got to feel the fear and take the action you're scared of.

So I'm going to be sharing with you my personal secret to getting your bum off the sofa and making your dreams a reality.

Here's a brief rundown of what I'll be getting you to do this week:

Day 8

We're going to take stock of your life and define what *really* needs to change, once and for all.

Day 9

We're going to get clear on your deepest desires and what you really want from your life.

Day 10

We will create your personal goal map, breaking your big goal into manageable bite-sized pieces.

Day 11

I'm going to invite you to join my Sunday Night Club, and show you the secret to my success.

Day 12

We're going to hire you some help, someone who is going to be supporting you over the coming months to help you get where you want to go.

Day 13

We'll be getting our hands dirty as we get cracking on making your dreams come alive.

Day 14

Your time for reflection and rest.

Day 8 – What's Not Working?

It's time to take a good hard look at your life. Now that you have uncovered your unique blueprint, and you have a better understanding about what makes you tick, it's time to stand back and look at your life with fresh eyes. *What's not working?* What continues to *challenge you?* What's *holding you back?* What *frustrates you?* What is making you most *unhappy?* What really *needs to change?* In order to fully apply ourselves and to know what our true desires are, we first have to be brave and wake up to what no longer serves us. Yeah, it's tough and sometimes even painful. But the fact is, you can't change your life until you're ready to acknowledge, let go and find solutions. It's just the way it is. As I always say, *awareness* is the key to change.

When you wake up to the fact that something isn't working anymore, whether that is your thinking patterns, your relationship, your business, your job, your money situation, and so on, you regain your power. You transform in an instant.

You fully step into your power and from this place
you can work miracles.

When you say to the Divine, *"Hey, I've had enough of this and I'm willing to see things differently and take action"*, miraculous solutions start to appear.

But if we continue to plod on unwilling to see the truth, our life stands still and we wind up feeling more disillusioned, frustrated and bitter. We become victims rather than creators. And we are here to co-create. This is our purpose, remember?

We are all here to design our life, but if our life is filled with stuff that isn't serving us, there is no room to create anything. Emotional, physical, spiritual, mental and energetic blocks can all get in the way of us living our best life.

So let me ask you: *"What do you need to change in your life right now?"*

Now, let me get clear on something. This isn't about acknowledging that you hate your job and immediately handing in your notice, or deciding that your boyfriend is a shit and suddenly ending your relationship by text. I'm not advocating that you run out and radically change everything right now, but I am encouraging you to wake up and smell the coffee. From this standpoint, you can then decide what your plan of action will be.

Sometimes instigating change takes time and careful planning, and sometimes it can happen pretty fast.

We live in changing times. There's an air of uncertainty, which is scary or exciting, depending on your viewpoint. We are being challenged to evolve to the next level and reach our fullest potential. *This is why you're reading this book.* The Divine is nudging you! Our natural setting is to stay the same, to remain safe and comfortable with what we know. This setting guards our wellbeing and that's a good thing. Yet it is those who take risks and make changes (even the very small ones) that are the most successful in health, wealth and love. So why is it often so difficult?

Change is difficult because we are programmed to fear the worst. We are creatures of habit. We get used to our routine and accept a particular way of being. This seems to get worse the older we get. Of course, many people are content with the way things are, but change opens up new doors of opportunity that we may not have even considered.

Being willing to change allows miracles to come into our life.

There are two ways of looking at change. The first is that you are in charge of making a change. You decide what you want and you make it happen. Even if it's a bit scary, you are taking the reins and that's exhilarating. What often happens when we don't change is that change is forced upon us in some way. We may be waiting for that to happen, for somebody else to take the responsibility, or it may happen when we least expect it. Either way, we will have to adapt to the change whether we like it or not. Which way sounds preferable?

Change is a natural part of the human growth process. Look back and consider all of the changes that have happened in your life, from school to your first job, to all your friendships and relationships. Think about how the world has changed and how you have adapted to those changes, and the valuable lessons that you have learned along the way. What can be perceived as a negative change, e.g., relationship breakdowns and redundancy can turn out to be blessings in disguise, although tremendously painful at the time. Sometimes we have to *let go of the old* to *let the new in.*

Often, not wanting to change relates to not wanting to get out of our comfort zone, or not having to confront or hurt somebody else's feelings. These are admirable traits, but it's so important that we put our own happiness, health and wellbeing first. This might seem selfish, but once we start to become happier, those around us will soon (or eventually) follow. Sometimes, we feel deep down that we are not worthy of better things, whether that's a better job, relationship or lifestyle. Once we start making small changes, we'll naturally start to attract the great things we do deserve. *Remember, when you shine, you give others permission to shine, too.*

I remember the day I decided that I'd had enough of my job as a marketing manager. I felt undervalued, uninspired and totally apathetic. Every day was the same and I could do it standing on my head! I would mope about my office whining to anyone who would listen, and by the end of the day I had no energy to do anything other than slob out in front of the TV. I wasn't being fair to my boss and I wasn't being fair to myself. What once served me well had lost its allure. I had outgrown it. I was outstaying my welcome and the Divine was trying to let me know that it was time to move on. The Universe had a bigger plan in store, but it wasn't until I decided that enough was enough and I needed to find my spark again that the Divine started to show me an alternative path.

As humans, we have complete free will, but until we decide that we're ready to find a better way of life, the Divine cannot assist us.

My transition to being a business owner didn't happen overnight. I had to train, do my research and build the foundations of my business from the ground up. But I clearly remember after 12 months of hard work and planning, I walked into my boss's office on January 2 2008 and told him I was leaving to launch my business and write my first book. It was the most terrifying yet liberating moment of my life. Sometimes we have to get super brave, and be willing to look beyond our current paradigm to take that leap of faith.

None of this would have happened if I had of decided to plod on. Fortunately I woke up, and decided that I was worth more. I started to communicate with the Divine and undertook a voyage of discovery to find out what living my full potential really looked like. Thank goodness I did.

What a journey it has been, and it all started from that one decision that I was ready to make a change.

So, today is *all about* taking stock of your life. I have devised some really poignant questions that will help you to start thinking about what needs to change in your life.

 Today's Assignment:

Take some time out to answer the following questions:

1) What's not working in your life right now?
2) What continues to challenge you?
3) What's holding you back?
4) What frustrates you the most?
5) What is making you most unhappy?
6) What really needs to change?
7) How would you like to see things change in 12 months' time?

A prayer for today:

"Although I feel scared and unsure about my future and what's next for me, I ask for your guidance. Please increase my faith and show me the way. Thank you."

Day 9 – Your Deepest Desires

Did you know that according to a recent university study, individuals who write down their goals earn nine times more in their lifetime than those who don't? This statistic really caught my eye. Aside from the money aspect, it shows that we can achieve more by getting *clear on our goals.* This has been my experience personally, and it is certainly the case when I'm coaching my private clients.

Here's why. Firstly, when we articulate and get clear about our desires, we start to really focus on what we're trying to accomplish. We create plans and begin to take baby steps in the right direction. *Our energy starts moving toward our goals.* Also, when we write our goals down and get totally clear, the Divine hears our call and gets into action, too.

This is about bringing the spiritual and the practical together so magic can happen. You can't manifest what you really want unless you know what that looks like. You need to see it in your imagination first. When you get clear about your desires and intentions, the Divine can provide you with all the little gems you need to move forward towards your goals. You'll start meeting the right people, receiving welcome emails or letters, and stumbling across the books or workshops that can help you in your quest.

We don't have to figure it all out at once, we just have to keep our frequency high, remain focused and stay open to the signs.

It's time to start communicating with the Universe so you can get clear on what you really want!

Exciting, eh? Or maybe this is more terrifying than exciting!

I want good solid rock-your-world kind of goals. We are not talking pesky New Year's resolutions here, such as going to the gym more, eating less dairy or buying a new carpet for your bedroom, everyone wants that kind of stuff. We're talking big, juicy scary goals that are going to get the fire burning inside your soul again. *We're talking about living your purpose.* It's time to find your power and step up.

I need you to suspend your belief about what you think is possible at this time, and open up to the possibility that the Divine has the power to bring you what you want. In truth, the Divine can give you everything you need; it's our beliefs about what we think is achievable that limit us.

Did you know that *'I am clear'* is an anagram for *'a miracle'*? Being clear is about being really specific about what you want to achieve, what changes you want to make, and seeing them in your mind's eyes. When you're clear, all the energies of the Universe can come together to deliver what you're wanting. It really is that simple. It's only our doubt and disbelief that stops our dreams from manifesting in physical form.

Think about it like this. If you were to send an email to your friend, you wouldn't send a jumbled up sentence of letters and expect him or her to be able to translate your message. You would of course send a coherent sentence that meant something. When deciding what you want in life, you've got to get totally clear, otherwise the Divine won't be able to decode your message and you won't get what you want.

Up until the age of 25, I hadn't got a clue about the power of intention and manifestation. I had a good life and had been pretty lucky with jobs, but I just put my blessings down to luck. But when I started reading about the concept of co-creation and how what we focus on expands, something deep within me stirred and I knew I was on to something. So I decided to put the theory to the test. And being an all or nothing kind of gal, I was totally committed to my quest. If we could really manifest anything we wanted by communicating somehow with the Divine, then I didn't want to miss out. To me, it didn't make sense that some people where super rich, while others suffered without two pennies to rub together. I had always felt a pull towards something deeper. I sensed that there was some vital piece of the jigsaw missing, and it was at this point in my life that I woke up and found out what this was.

Within just a few short years, my life was unrecognisable. I had created a successful business from nothing and managed to run it around my family and the school run. I'd become a published author with a global publishing house, and I'd been invited to speak alongside my idols, Louise Hay and Dr. Wayne Dyer, and some of the world's most prominent self-help gurus. I even had dinner with Dr. Wayne Dyer, Sonia Choquette, Cheryl Richardson and Robert Holden. I'd been featured in almost all the national women's magazines and even founded an annual event called *International Change Your Life Week*. I had created so much in such a short space of time, which made me realise that the stuff I was reading about actually worked, and that I am pretty damned good at manifesting. Has it all been good luck? Of course not! Have I worked my arse off to get it? *Of course I have!*

But here's what I need you to hear:

'I have set very clear goals and I have taken constant action to get where I am. I have worked very hard, but I have also been riding in the flow of universal energy. I've had the Universe working on my behalf to bring people, things and opportunities into my life. I've done this by bringing the physical and spiritual together. I've set goals, followed the signs and taken action.'

I'm not saying this to boast. I am saying this to *inspire* and *encourage* you, because if I can do it, so can you. I am no more gifted or special than you are. We all have access to the same internal power. The only difference between someone who is living their full potential and someone who is not is that the former has discovered how to tap into the Divine Infinite Intelligence. They are riding in the flow. Are you?

I'm not asking you to take my word for gospel, but I am asking you to wake up and become your *own* scientist. Learn to tap in and ride in the flow. Do this, and you too will discover your own truth. Getting what you want in life starts with deciding what *you* want! We are creators, and we are here to use our imagination to create what we desire. This is your purpose and what the Divine wants for you. Living a small life is wasting the power that you've been given. You are a creator and you can create miracles.

But here is the problem that most people come up against. You set your intentions, you write your goals down and you pray and meditate. The Divine hears your call and all the forces of the Universe come together to deliver your request. It's quite literally on its way to you. It's in touching distance. But then normal life kicks in and you lose your focus and faith. Your inner critic wades in and negative thoughts besiege you and squish your dreams. As the outer world appears more real than the inner, you start to doubt yourself. This is your demise. You unconsciously push your dreams away again. You put a halt on the Divine flow. This leads to a constant game of cat and mouse because you never quite allow yourself to reach the prize. You never quite allow the Universe to deliver your big dream.

The key to co-creating is *staying focused* and keeping your frequency *super high*. When you learn how to do this, you will be able to manifest at super speed and you'll find that no sooner have you thought of something, it appears in your life.

I will be teaching you how to keep your frequency high by creating a daily practice later on in this book.

For now, here's what I want you to do. I want you to imagine that 12 months has passed and you've had the most amazing year of your life. You've achieved some awesome things and you're now looking back and reviewing your year. What do you see? What changes have occurred? Take a look at each area of your life, from work to love and home, and notice the positive changes that have taken place. Don't lose yourself in the details of how you got there, and don't allow doubt and disbelief to creep in, just see the end vision.

So today I want to get you *thinking about your year ahead and what you'd really like to achieve in the next 12 months.*

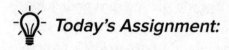 *Today's Assignment:*

Today you are going to set yourself a big, juicy life-changing goal. Be clear, succinct and positive.

Use the following questions to help you along.

1) Did you have a childhood dream? If so, what was it?
2) What are you passionate about in life?
3) If you had no limitations such as money, or lack of qualifications, what would you love to do?
4) What long lost dreams have you been putting on the back burner for the past five, 10 or 15 years?
5) What is missing from your life currently?
6) Is there anything that you've seen on the telly, read in a magazine, or heard a friend or colleague talking about that has sparked your interest recently? If so, what was it?
7) What's the *one thing* you want to do before you die?
8) What goal could you set which would make the *biggest difference* to your life?

Decide on what your big goal is, write it down and pin it on a wall where you'll see it often. Declare your goal to the Universe!

Day 10 – Your Road Map

When it comes to setting big, juicy life-changing goals, here's where most people fall down. Firstly, they think that setting a goal is enough, and they forget to take any *action*. Or secondly, they set their goal and then quickly become totally overwhelmed by trying to do too much too soon.

I've tried both approaches, and neither work! You need to take a sensible and pragmatic approach to your goals. But also look out for the signs and signals from the Universe along the way.

Remember, this is about learning to bring the *practical and the spiritual together*. The Divine can and will assist you on your journey to achieving your goals, but you've got to get your bum off the sofa and take consistent and steady action. Some goals can manifest super quick, others take longer.

You can rub crystals, meditate and drink green smoothies all day long, but unless you get your running shoes on and start jogging, you're not going to get to the finish line. We may be spiritual beings, but let's not forget that we are also living in a very real and physical world, which requires us to move *physical matter* in order to manifest want we want. We've got to go to class, make that phone call, write that email and go on that first date. There's no other way around it!

I've worked with thousands of people over the last eight years and shared with them a simple yet powerful formula for achieving goals. Over the next few days, I'll also be revealing this to you.

First off, you need to create your *goal map*. This is like a road map, but it sets out a strategy for where you are going and how you are going to get there. Basically, this is a high level overview of all the milestones that you are going to need to reach in order to achieve your goal. When I work with my private clients, this is one of the first things that we do. Creating a goal map breaks your aims down, allowing you to focus on them one at a time, rather than trying to do everything at once.

If you don't create a goal map it's like deciding that you're going to climb Mount Everest in one day. You're setting yourself up to fail. You need to plan your route, get fully equipped, get support and take steady baby steps. This way you'll reach the summit with ease and enjoy the journey to the top far more.

Having a goal map isn't about planning out every single action in advance (this would be impossible and would totally go against the laws of manifesting), but it is about chunking your goals down into *manageable* pieces and creating a *timeline*.

For example, when I'm about to write a book, rather than just sitting down one day with a blank piece of paper, I take a little time to map out my journey. I decide on the name and theme of my book, and then I flesh out each section. I then create a writing schedule so that I have a deadline for each section to be written by. My next step is the actual writing of each chapter, before finally submitting my manuscript to my publisher. These are clear milestones for me to reach. It's far better to have a rough breakdown than to blindly head into a big goal and end up feeling lost or overwhelmed.

When we feel besieged and fearful, we give up on our dreams and fail to turn them into reality. So be gentle on yourself.

Remember, you can't climb Everest in a day!

Something very interesting happens when we start to take action towards our goals. We start to get signs, signals and clues from the Universe, which help us move forward. I call this the *Divine Matrix*. We can't ever fathom out how the Divine Matrix works, all we can do is trust it and take the next Divinely guided step. While we can't possibly know every action we'll need to take in advance, we can create a very simple goal map that outlines the basic milestones we'll need to reach in order to achieve it. This helps us stay focused and gives our goal depth and structure.

So when I set myself a big goal, such as writing a new book, creating a new online course, mastering a skill, or completing a decorating project at home, the first thing I do is set a date for when I want to reach this goal. It could be three months, six months, or as long as a year. I then brainstorm all the milestones I'll need to reach along my journey. I then put my milestones in order and put a dates next to each one. And finally I put my goal map on my office wall. *It's that simple.*

When you do this, your focus is only on your current milestone. You're not rushing ahead, or trying to accomplish all your milestones in one go. You're just focusing on one step at a time. This may not be rocket science, but it is how to make big things happen in your life – one step at a time.

So today you are going to take the goal that you set yesterday and create your own goal map, plus a series of milestones that you'll need to achieve in order to reach it. Don't set yourself more than 10 milestones or it becomes too overwhelming and scary. It can really be helpful to have someone to brainstorm with, so recruit a supportive friend to help you do this.

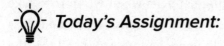 *Today's Assignment:*

Today you are going to create your goal map:

1) Set an end date for your goal.
2) Now create your goal map. Remember, these are just simple milestones to help you break your goal down into bite-sized pieces.
3) Pin your goal map on your wall alongside your big goal.
4) Set the intention that in advance of your goal you will not try to figure out every action that you'll need to take. (By doing this you will get in the way of the Universe delivering what you need and miss the miracle.) Instead, focus on the one milestone in front of you.

Don't future trip, stay in the present.

Day 11 - Join The Sunday Night Club!

Do you want to know the secret to my success in life so far? Yes? Brace yourself; this one is going knock your socks off!

I write a *'to do'* list each and every week. Okay, so it didn't quite knock you off your seat, but seriously, this really is the secret to me achieving so much in the last few years. Having a *'to do'* list keeps me focused on where I'm going, but, most importantly, it stretches me *to take* those vitally important baby steps.

As Kris Carr, New York Times bestselling author and wellness activist says: *"If you want to be a game changer, you first have to be an action taker!"*

While your goal map is more of an overview, actions are specific steps that you need to take in order to achieve your current milestone.

Actions are the engine to your dreams, and they bring your desires into physical form. Nothing materialises in this world without manpower (and womanpower, of course!). The Divine won't write your book for you, and it won't fill in that application form or mail that letter. Of course, the Divine will assist us to a point, but we are the ones who have to take action in the real world. This is where, if we're not careful, we can miss out on the miracles and bounty that life has to offer.

The Divine is constantly trying to communicate with us, and give us signs and signals. It continually brings us the teachers, the books and the opportunities, but very often we turn our back on this Divine guidance and miss the miracle. We literally lean away from the light just when we need it the most.

Have you ever had an awesome idea that you were too scared to take action on, only to find out that someone else took the idea and ran with it? I know I have. When the Divine delivers guidance that you're not prepared to act on, it simply passes on that guidance to another person who is willing to say *'yes'*. The Divine never gives up on you, and there's always fresh guidance coming your way, but why wait and waste time when you could start living your purpose today?

Start leaning into the light and stay there.

Each Sunday evening, I think about the coming week and all the things that I need to focus on. I meditate and pray for guidance, and then ask for clarity on my actions. My *'to do'* list is quite literally Divinely guided. I ask for anything that is not the best use of my talent to be cast from my mind (and *'to do'* list) and for actions that are the best use of my talent to be made clear.

With my list created, I wake up on Monday morning knowing exactly what I'm doing. Plus, because I check-in and continue to keep my frequency high, I know that each action I take is the right one to help me reach my goal.

I trust that each action I take will lead to the next action, and the next. I allow the Divine Matrix to work its magic. While I am aware of my bigger goal and my goal map, I am only ever focusing on the next baby step. This keeps me present. And it's in the present moment that transformation happens!

The great Steve Jobs, co-founder of Apple, shared this wonderful statement during his Stanford Commencement speech in 2005.
"You can't connect the dots looking forward; you can only connect

them looking backwards. So you have to trust that the dots will somehow connect in your future. You have to trust in something – your gut, destiny, life, karma, whatever. Because believing that the dots will connect down the road will give you the confidence to follow your heart even when it leads you off the well-worn path; and that will make all the difference."

Every action you take connects the dots.

In my own life, I am constantly in detective mode. I am always looking at how things fit into the bigger picture. I never dismiss an email, a conversation or an opportunity until I've checked-in with myself. Discernment is the name of my game. When you're connected, you know when something is the right thing to do, and, conversely, you also know when something isn't. This is why we must stay connected (I'll be showing you how to do this shortly). The more *connected* you are, the clearer and more accurate the guidance you receive will be.

When things go pear shaped in my life, I know that somewhere along the line I became disconnected and made a decision from a place of anxiety and fear.

I have total faith that the disturbance I'm experiencing is just the Divine's way of putting me back on track.

Daily, clients drop me emails to tell me about the amazing things that have happened to them. I'm always astounded by the incredible synchronicities that come into play when people get serious about changing their lives. Your own guidance might come in the form of a comment someone says that resonates deeply with you. It might come by way of an email, a letter, by visiting a specific location, or by bumping into an old friend. The Divine is a complex matrix and can move heaven and earth to help us manifest our desires, but we've got to be wide eyed and bushy tailed so we don't miss the miracle. Quite often, the clues can be so subtle that they don't make it on to our radar. But fortunately, the Divine doesn't give up that easily. It'll keep tapping you on your shoulder, or banging you over the head if necessary, until you finally take heed, listen and act.

One thing I've come to know for sure is this:

'Successful people take action even before they are ready.'

Personally, this is also how I live my life. When I know that something feels right, even though I may feel scared, I say *'yes'*. And these *'yeses'* have turned out to be the biggest blessings of my life.

Divinely guided action is the name of the game.

Without action, *nothing* will change. With all the good intentions in the world, you need to get used to stepping out of your comfort zone. It's often said that your life begins outside of this, and I think this is very true. All of my clients have to expand beyond theirs in order to live their dreams. This is a requirement for all the clients that work with me. If they're not prepared to change and extend their comfort zone, then it'll never work. It's just the way it is. In order to stop being a sheep, we have to venture away from the familiar surroundings of our flock. We have to forge our own new path through unfamiliar territory, and this invariably means that the terrain can sometimes be scary and challenging. But in order to get to the promised land, in order to bring our dreams into reality, we have to get committed and we have to step up. And most importantly, we have to take responsibility and *take action*.

 ## Today's Assignment:

Today we are going to establish a brand new habit.

Come join the Sunday Night Club.

Every week (starting this week), you are going to create your divinely guided *'to do'* list. Before you begin writing, take a second to connect with your inner guide (your intuition), and ask, *"What action do I need to take this week?"* Sit quietly for a few moments and listen. If nothing comes through write your list anyway and then say, *"Please cast from my mind (and to do list) anything that is not the right action for me to take this week. For actions that are the best use of my talent, please keep me focused and on track."*

Make a note every Sunday in your diary to write your *'to do'* list for the week ahead. Do this and It. Will. Change. Your. Life.

Remember, actions are the engine to your dreams!

Day 12 – Help!

When we are supported by like-minded souls, it makes for a much easier and enjoyable ride. We are social creatures and we need to interact with other human beings for our general wellbeing and peace of mind.

We've all experienced times when, for whatever reason, we've spent far too much time alone and haven't seen anyone for days. It doesn't feel good, does it? Now some people are social butterflies and like to constantly be surrounded by other people, while others are more than happy to spend lots of time alone. Wherever you are on this scale, it's still important to remember that we need to communicate and share our feelings with other like-minded people. It keeps our vibrations high. And when are vibrations are high, we are magnets attracting miracles from every direction.

So now that you have set your big goal and created your plan of action, we're going to focus on recruiting help.

One thing I know for sure is that we are a nation of procrastinators:

'We'll do it tomorrow, next month, when we get paid, when we get back from our holiday, when the kids are grown up, when the boss pops his clogs - you know the score. We love to put things off to some bright sunny day in the distant future when everything is just perfect. But invariably, that bright sunny perfect day never materialises.'

Have you ever experienced a time when you were in a quandary and just couldn't make a decision? Yes? Have you ever noticed that when you speak with a friend and seek their advice, the right way often becomes clear?

Using our intuition is awesome and really helps us to take the correct route, but sometimes we just need to talk it through with another human being.

Very recently, I was considering signing up to an online course. It wasn't cheap, but what concerned me the most was the time and input that it would require. I agonised for almost a week about whether to do it or not. It wasn't until I'd spoken to someone else who'd already signed up to the course, that I realised it wasn't the right time for me to get involved. This one five-minute conversation helped me to make my decision. Sometimes, other human beings are Divinely put in our path to communicate a message to us. Very often, when we are not listening to our internal guidance, the Divine has to take a different route and send in a human to set us straight.

Working towards big goals solo can be lonely, and without the love and support of others it's very easy to lose faith and give up. Having a shoulder to cry on when things don't go as planned, or someone to celebrate with when you get your biggest breakthrough can make *all* the difference as to whether you fail or succeed.

Those who are successful glean help from others, whether that's by getting assistance from family or friends, hiring an expert or creating some kind of mastermind group. Either way, having helps rocks!

For the first three years of my business I did everything myself, and I mean *everything*. I coached, planned, marketed, sold, filled in my tax return, sorted out my accounts and my admin, made my own tea, cleaned my house, washed my car, decorated my own woodwork and, of course, I took care of my gorgeous brood.

Phew! It was hard work keeping all those balls in the air. But I was under the misguided impression that this is what a *'modern'* woman has to do. Then one day, I had a complete hissy fit. I decided that I wasn't some kind of superwoman and threw all my balls down! I concluded that I would only retain the balls that I liked juggling, and I'd give the remaining ones to someone else to juggle instead. *This was a huge turning point in my life and my business.*

I hired a mentor, a PA, a bookkeeper and an accountant. I also employed someone to help me with my PR, a social media expert and a branding guru. I hired a cleaner and started taking my car to the carwash. I stopped trying to take on the world and realised that I needed to stay in my gift zone. Ok, I didn't hire all these people in one fell swoop, but slowly but surely I allowed myself to let go and only focus on what I was really good at: motherhood, coaching, marketing and making an excellent brew!

God put other people on this planet so that we can all collaborate and help each other. We don't have to take on the world single handedly, and we certainly don't have to ride solo! Where's the fun it that?

One word of warning. We must recruit the *right* people to help and support us. As much as family and friends love and care for us, they don't always understand our mission and goal. They have their own opinion about what they think we should or shouldn't do, and if we're not careful this can get in our way.

We've all experienced a time when we've been super excited about something, only for someone close to pour icy cold water on our ideas. It's a horrible feeling. It's *essential* that you choose the *right people* to support you on your journey. Very often this is why people hire coaches and mentors - because they are impartial and 100% focused on their clients.

When you think about recruiting the perfect person to help you on your journey, keep in mind the following points:

- ✓ You want someone with a naturally high vibration.
- ✓ You want someone like-minded who understands you and shares your enthusiasm for your goal.
- ✓ You want someone who is solution focused, not someone who will wallow in self-pity with you!
- ✓ You want someone who is available to help and willing to have a regular conversation with you.
- ✓ If a friend is helping you for free, consider doing a skills swap. It's vitally important that you are both clear on boundaries before you start.
- ✓ Also, consider who can help you create more time to focus on your new goals: a cleaner, babysitter, gardener, etc.

 Today's Assignment:

Make a list of the people in your life that can help you with your goal.

Think about current and former work colleagues, local businesses, family, friends, neighbours, coaches, mentors, experts, therapists, specialists, gurus, consultants, healers, teachers, and so on. If you can't think of anyone, get yourself on Auntie Google!

Then make contact and ask for help.

Remember, you don't have to do this *alone*. The Divine wants you to be successful and if you ask it will provide exactly the right people to assist you on your journey.

Day 13 – Let's Step Into Your Time Machine

Today, we're going to have some fun! Pictures are the universal language of the soul. The world is created through mental image. What you see in your mind's eye materialises into the pictures of your life. This is creation in motion and the law of the Universe. In order to successfully co-create our deepest desires, we have to get clear about our intentions and goals, and we have to take the necessary action to move towards them. But the one thing that keeps our frequency high and keeps us in universal flow is remaining steadfast to our big vision.

Napoleon Hill, an American author in the area of the New Thought movement once said: *"Whatever the mind can conceive and believe, it can achieve."*

I have been travelling on my Divine path for a little while now, and what I know for sure, without any doubt, is that when I am passionate about what I'm wanting, and when I play this image in my mind with great conviction, I know I will manifest it into my life very soon.

So today we are going to create your future in images. We are going raise your vibrations and get you all fired up and excited about what you're about to create in your life. *We are going to create your dream board.*

Creating Your Dream Board

What is a dream board?

A dream board (also called a vision board, mood board,

treasure map or creativity collage) is typically a poster board on which you paste a collection of images that you've torn from various magazines or found online. It's very simple. The idea behind it is that when you surround yourself with images of who you want to become, what you want to have, where you want to live or where you want to go on holiday, your life changes to match those images and desires. The Divine hears your call, plus it's so much more creative than just writing your goal down and sticking it on the wall.

To create your own dream board you'll need:

➤ Some sturdy card, the bigger the better.
➤ A pile of different magazines. Ensure that you find lots of different types. If you limit your options you'll lose interest after a while. Ask family and friends for their old magazines.
➤ Scissors.
➤ Glue stick, coloured pens and maybe a bit of glitter!!

The five steps of creating a dream board

Step 1) Go through your magazines and tear out any images that strike your fancy. You can also source images online, too. No gluing just yet, just let yourself have lots of fun looking through magazines and pulling out the pictures, or even words and headlines, that catch your eye. Have fun with it. Make a big pile of images, phrases and words that really call out to you.

Step 2) Go through the images and begin to place your favourite ones on the board. Scrap any images that no longer feel right. This is where your intuition comes in. As you lay the pictures on the board, you'll get a sense of how it should be laid out. For instance, you might assign a theme to each corner of the board, with a section for health, work, spirituality and relationships. Or it may be that the images want to go all over the place.

Step 3) Glue everything on to the board. If you want, add writing, colour and glitter. You can paint on it, or write words with markers.

Step 4) This dream board it all about you, so it makes sense for you to make space for a fab photo of yourself looking radiant and happy. Paste yourself in the centre of your board. This is the most important step!

Step 5) Hang your dream board in a place where you will see it often. The kitchen or bathroom usually works best.

> *Each time you pass your dream board, it will naturally give you a boost and raise your vibrations a little higher.*

There are two types of dream board that you can create. I'll share them with you before you get cracking.

1. The Intuitive Dream Board

Do this dream board if...

- ★ You're not sure exactly what you want.
- ★ You have a vision of what you want, but are uncertain about it in some way.
- ★ You know you want change but don't know how it's possible

How to create this dream board:

Go through each magazine and tear out any images that delight you. Don't ask why - just keep using your intuition. If it's a picture of a teddy bear that makes you smile, then pull it out. If it's a cottage in the countryside, then rip that out. Just have fun and be open to whatever calls to you. When you have selected your images or words, stick them on your board and ask yourself what each picture or word might mean. What is it telling you? Does it mean that you need to take more time for yourself? Does it mean that you want to get a dog, or stop hanging out with a particular person who drains you? Most likely, you'll know the answer. But don't worry if you don't, it will come to you soon enough. The Intuitive Dream Board can be a powerful guide for you. It's your soul talking to you through pictures. This is my favourite type of board because sometimes our ego thinks it knows what we want, and a lot of the time those desires aren't in alignment with our blueprint. This board goes deeper, and that's why I love it so much.

2. The Themed Dream Board

Do this dream board if...

★ You are focusing on one particular area of your life. For instance, work, business, motherhood, home improvement.

How to create this dream board:

The only difference between this vision board and the other one is that this one has clear parameters and intent. Before you begin, take a moment to hold the intent and the theme/goal in mind.

When you choose pictures, they will be in alignment with this theme.

 Today's Assignment:

Make sure that you have what you need before you start:

This includes board or card, magazines, glue, scissors, and so on. Find some quiet time, get on the floor and get cutting and gluing.
   Have fun creating your dream board!

Day 14 – Your Day for Reflection And Rest

Take time today to let what have learned this week sink in.

Also, take a couple of minutes to answer the following questions:

1) What *insights* have your gained about yourself this week?
2) What have you *discovered* about yourself that you weren't aware of before?
3) How are you *feeling* about what you have learned?
4) How might this *change* your life for the better?
5) What is the most *important* thing you must now do?

Prayer for this week:

"Dear Divine Guidance, even though I feel scared right now, I am willing to release and let go of all that no longer serves me. Thank you for helping me to make this process as easy as possible. Thank you for helping me to bring my dreams and ambitions to reality and for guiding me towards a path that will fill my life with peace and joy. I welcome new people and opportunities into my life with open arms. Thank you for keeping me strong and focused during these times of change."

And so it is.

WEEK 3

DAYS 15-21

Mastering Your Mind

Days 15-21

Mastering Your Mind

I remember reading my first spiritual self-development book, *Excuse Me, Your Life Is Waiting*, by an author called Lynn Grabhorn, and being deeply excited by its content. Half of me rejected everything she said as total rubbish, the other half was jumping up and down in delight.

It was as if she had just handed me the key to my freedom.

In my heart, I knew after reading this book that my life was never going to be the same again. There was no going back; I couldn't take back the knowledge that had been imparted. My mind was racing in all directions, and, for the first time in my life, I was allowing myself to dream big. I had opened the door to a new world and even if I had wanted to, I didn't know how to shut it again. I had no choice but to take my new found knowledge and put it to action.

I remember thinking to myself that if all this thoughts-create-your-reality was really genuine, then I was going to have to put it to the test and apply it to my life. I followed every technique suggested, and completed every exercise offered. My determination and commitment was irrefutable. I wanted change and I promised myself that if this happened, I would make it my life's mission to share the knowledge I'd learned.

The girl that once sat on the sofa, cup of tea in one hand, trashy novel in the other, was now reading books about neuroscience and quantum physics. This raised a few eyebrows, and I could sense that my family was worried about my transformation; I could see it in their perplexed faces. All of sudden I was using words like *'manifest'*, *'the Universe'* and *'divine guidance'*. They looked at me in total puzzlement as I tried desperately to share my new-found passion with them. I was challenging their perceptions of how their world worked, and they really didn't like it.

I began plastering my house with Post-it notes with positive affirmative statements written on them. I joined a local meditation class and went off to lectures and seminars on my own. I was no longer the same girl, but I LOVED the new girl that was emerging.

I had never felt so alive in my entire life.

The more I practised changing my mindset, the more I started to notice changes happening in my life. They were all subtle to start with, but transformation was most definitely afoot. I started to feel more empowered and optimistic. I had more energy and felt a natural desire to want learn and grow. Amazing ideas and insights came to me on a regular basis. My life was changing before my eyes. It was like a light switch had been switched on inside me, and I was shining bright for the first time in my life.

Within 18 months, my life was unrecognisable. I had trained in a brand new profession, left my employed job to start a business from home and was writing my first book. Fast-forward eight years and I am now one of the UK's leading personal growth experts with a thriving practice. I am also a published author, speak on stage, write for magazines and inspire people worldwide with my work. Not so long ago, this was a pipe dream. My intention isn't to brag, but what I do want to demonstrate is that with the right mindset, you too can achieve your dreams, whatever they may be. *And this week it's my aim to show you how.*

The truth is that it's much easier for people to believe that they don't have any control over their life whatsoever. It's so much easier to blame the government for your lack of career prospects, or to accuse your boss for holding you down in your job. Playing the victim means that we don't have to take responsibility for our lives. And in doing so we stay small.

Yet we all have much more power than we can possibly conceive of. The Divine Infinite Intelligence is just waiting for us all to wake up and take responsibility for our lives, because when we do we literally open a door into a new world.

So this week, I'm taking you on a journey into your mind.

We're going to take charge of your life and really understand what's been holding you back. We'll look at those innermost thoughts and beliefs that get in the way of you reaching your full potential.

I am going to show you how to change your mind and reprogram your thinking with four *seriously powerful techniques.*

Here's a brief rundown of what I'll be getting you to do this week:

Day 15

Meet your *inner guide*, which acts as your heavenly support.

Day 16

Meet your *inner critic*, the negative voice within that is sabotaging your dreams.

Day 17

We're going to *open the channel* and really become aware of how thoughts and beliefs shape your life.

Day 18

It's time to shine a light on the *three big beliefs* that have been holding you back.

Day 19

We're going to create *three new shiny beliefs* that are going to shape your new future.

Day 20

I'm going to share *four techniques* to help reprogram your mind, once and for all.

Day 21

Your time for reflection and rest.

Day – 15 Your Inner Guide

Everyone on this planet has access to his or her own inner power - the *Divine Infinite Intelligence*. Nobody is without access, it's your birthright. Whether you use it or not is a different matter. Human beings have complete free will to believe and do what they choose.

I believe that everyone has a team of spiritual helpers to assist them in tapping into the Divine Infinite Intelligence. What you call your spiritual helpers is totally up to you, but it helps if you can refer to them in a way that makes you feel comfortable and at ease. You could call them God, the force, your higher self, your inner guide, your gut, your intuition, your angels, your sixth sense, your vibes... the list is endless. There is no right or wrong. You decide.

But without a doubt, there is a Divine Infinite Intelligence within you, which, when tapped into, will lead you directly to your life's purpose and result in all the riches you could ever want or need.

I like referring to my inner power as my Inner Guide. One of my clients prefers to call hers Secret Fairy, and another is happy to use the term God. Use whatever term feels true for you. Now it's time for you to join forces with your inner power so that you too can access the infinite possibilities that the Divine provides.

Your *inner guide* (or whichever term you like to use for your inner power) knows you inside out. She's been there since the day you were born, loving you intensely without you even knowing. She's watched you grow inch by inch; greeted you at the school gates, helped you find the courage to stand up to the school bully and she soothed your anguish the first time your heart was broken. She knows you better than anyone else in your life, even down to nitty-gritty detail of how you like your coffee in the morning and what your favourite song is. She is also aware of all the thoughts that whirl around in the deep, dark crevices of your mind. But most importantly, she knows who you are underneath all the fictitious layers of habits, beliefs and behaviours that you've acquired over the years. She knows *exactly* who you are and what you came here to do, and she will guide you, step-by-step, back to your authentic self. But she can't help you if you're not listening. She will illuminate the way only if you let her, bringing people, circumstances and even Prince Charming directly into your path.

In short, she will move heaven and earth to ensure that you fulfill your purpose and find happiness.

Because we have been living our lives totally switched off and unaware of the magic at our fingertips, we believe that we must control everything around us, including our partner, boss, money and friends. We believe that we must fend for ourselves because there isn't enough to go around, and what we have got will either run out or be taken from us.

We survive in a competitive, fear-based and cut-throat planet. We become our own God as we believe that we know best. This distorted belief system has led us to manifest a sunny-side-down kind of life. A world that is lost and gripped by fear is a cruel one. Look around and see for yourself. It's plain to see. But isn't it truly liberating to know that there might be a better way? Slowly but surely, the world is waking up and people are realising that fear and greed isn't the truth of who we are.

Each person who wakes up to this helps the next person to do the same. The world is slowly shifting, one person at a time. The more people who learn to tap into the Divine Infinite Intelligence, the more our world will transform in front of our eyes.

Working in partnership with your inner guide and the Divine Infinite Intelligence, and trusting that there is a bigger plan, alleviates the pressure to have to control everything in your life. You can loosen your grip on life and relax knowing that you are exactly where you should be. It's not easy to begin with. Letting go of a lifetime of programming is terrifying. In many ways, it feels like you are losing yourself, and that your old life is falling away. But this isn't the case. You are simply emerging from the undergrowth to greet a new world.

I live every day of my life in constant dialogue with my own inner guide. I start my day with a meditation in which I ask for guidance. For every action I take, I stop and take a second to check-in and ask, *"Does this action feel right?"* I don't always get it right. I am human and I make mistakes, but I know in my heart that what I have achieved over the last few years is because I've learned how to tap into the Divine Infinite Intelligence. Remember, when you're tapped in, you get all the knowledge, ideas, solutions, wisdom and understanding that you need to live a magnificent life. It's like switching on a light in a darkened room. All of a sudden you can see everything clearly. You can't see when you're rooting around in the dark. Find the light switch and let's switch the damned light on!

My connection with my inner guide is a quiet union. It's a knowing that I must not try to control or stress about the outcome of things in my life. When I feel stressed or anxious, I shut off and can no longer connect with my inner power. So, instead of stressing, I simply hand it over and I say, *"Hey this is too big for me to figure out. I let go, I hand it to you, please sort it for me."* And she does. She never fails to amaze me. A solution manifests out of nowhere, an idea presents itself, or I get clarity on my next step. Nothing is beyond the Divine Infinite Intelligence. We just need to get out of our own way and let our inner guide assist us.

My inner guide is quite simply my best friend and, with her at my side, I never need look outside of myself for answers or approval. I just go within and connect.

For Christmas, I was given a very beautiful, not to mention expensive, pair of designer beige suede gloves, which I cherished. They were gorgeous, soft to the touch and a perfect match to my favourite coat. A few days after Christmas, I wore my lovely new gloves on a trip into town to run my usual errands.

I had the children with me and, as you can imagine, shopping with them can be somewhat frantic at the best of times. Quite often, it's even traumatic. Somewhere between the bank and the butchers, I lost one of my beautiful gloves. Gone. Disappeared. Vanished. I was devastated. I hadn't even had them on for five minutes and I'd managed to lose one! I went back down the high street, followed my footsteps and asked in all the shops we'd been in, but all this was to no avail. I finally had to admit defeat and return home with my one lonely glove.

In the car on the way back, my daughter, sensing how upset I was, tentatively asked, *"Mummy, why don't we say a little prayer to God and the angels and ask them to find your glove and keep it safe?"* My heart melted, and the anguish of my lost glove immediately dissolved. We said a little prayer asking that the glove be found and returned to mummy, and then we forgot about it.

Fast-forward three weeks. We were in the card shop choosing a birthday card for my father-in-law's 80th birthday. In the corner of my eye, I could sense the lady at the till staring at me. Feeling a little self-conscious, I turned to make eye contact. To my surprise, she ducked under the counter and pulled out a lonesome beige glove (yes my glove!).

"Did you by any chance lose a glove a few weeks ago?" She asked. *"Only we found it in the road and it was so nice that we couldn't just leave it there. So, we picked it up and put it to one side."*

I couldn't believe it. It was my beloved glove, and in perfect condition too! It turns out that it must have fallen off the buggy as we were rushing along. The shop assistant spotted it and picked it up for safekeeping.

The strange thing is, the shop assistant didn't know that it was my glove (we'd never met), but for some reason, call it intuition, a hunch or just plain old good luck, she knew it belonged to me as soon as I walked into the shop. How weird is that? Well, it's not really that weird if you're in tune with your inner power!

Well, you should have seen the face of my six-year-old. Appearing very wise and knowing, she looked up at me and very matter-of-factly said, *"I told you the angels would bring it back, Mummy."* In response, I leant down and kissed her little button nose. *How right she was!*

We have the ability to tap into our Divine guidance in all aspects of our lives. And the tale of my missing glove illustrates this perfectly. Be it a lost item, finding your way in life or discovering your true love. All we really need to do is ask… and then patiently wait.

I recall a recent phone conversation that I had with one of my private clients. We were discussing her connection with her own inner guide, which she called her sixth sense. She told me that she was aware of her sixth sense, but she only ever called upon it when times were tough and she was desperate. Most of the time her thoughts were governed by her negative inner critic. I asked her why she only ever called upon her sixth sense when she was desperate. She couldn't answer. I then asked her what the result would be if she tapped into her sixth sense every day, and not just when she was in need. The line went silent. I could hear the light bulb switch on in my client's head as she realised that she could actually tap in all the time, not just when things were tough. This was a *huge* turning point for her, and her life changed after that as a matter of course.

The more tapped in you are,
the clearer the guidance you'll receive.

So I'd like to ask you:

1) What does your inner power, or your inner guide, look like?
2) When you are feeling low, what message do you hear from your inner guide?
3) When you've had a breakthrough with something, what does your inner guide tell you?
4) What will happen if you tune in and connect with your inner guide more often?
5) How will this improve your life for the better?

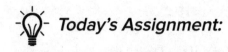 *Today's Assignment:*

I want you to spend a little time with your inner guide:

Take just five minutes, maybe in the morning or evening, maybe in the shower or on your drive to or from work, and say, *"hello"*. Feel the presence. What do you feel? What do you hear? It's subtle, but it's definitely there and it's definitely real. Just a few minutes a day will help strengthen your relationship with your inner guide.

Start today and make this a daily practice from this day forward.

Day 16 – Your Inner Critic

As we all have access to the glory of the *Divine Infinite Intelligence*, you might be wondering why everyone isn't already tapped in and manifesting all the riches the world has to offer. Why isn't everyone living their purpose, earning millions, driving around in a BMW and holidaying in Barbados?

Here's *why*. While each one of us is born *'connected'* to the Divine, we are literally ripped apart and programmed with a different version of reality that comes from our parents, siblings, teachers, religion and culture. We become carbon copies and our innate power is often switched off. We look to our peers to help us interpret life and form our version of reality. We are taught that we must conform and that we have no real power or control over our lives. These beliefs become our truth. These limitations become the limitations of our life. They become our glass ceiling.

They say that children are in an almost hypnotic state for the first few years of their lives. They are totally open to being programmed by those around them. If a child is constantly told that they are stupid or naughty, or not as attractive as their sister, or that there isn't enough money, then these beliefs get hardwired into their brain. And they take these negative beliefs into their adult lives.

By the time we reach adulthood, our subconscious is programmed with a myriad of negative and unhelpful beliefs that stop our inner guide, and ultimately the Divine Infinite Intelligence, from communicating with us. We unconsciously turn off our power. Our light slowly starts to dim and eventually switches off altogether, leaving us to live in the dark. Remember, we have complete free will. It is our birthright. So until we wake up and decide to reconnect, there is nothing our inner guide can do but wait for the call. Sadly, many people never make the call. They live their lives disconnected.

To help you understand this concept further and take control of your destiny, I'd like to introduce you to your inner critic.

Your inner critic, also known as your ego, is the tape that you play over and over again in your mind; it's your subconscious programming.

Most of us don't realise that we're being manipulated, controlled and held back by this negative voice within. In fact, most of us spend our entire day ruled by this voice alone. The constant whine of your inner critic will tell you, *"But you can't do that"/"They'll laugh at you"/"You're just not clever enough"/ "You'll never have enough money"/"He won't look twice at you."* These messages become the mantra of our lives.

This is a *major epidemic* in our society today. It keeps people totally stuck within their current paradigm. We have a world full of people *'playing small'*. A world of gifted, talented and amazing individuals who believe that somehow they're just not good enough, that their opinion doesn't count, that they're not attractive enough, or that they're somehow living a lie. Sound familiar?

As a child my inner critic would take pleasure in reminding me how stupid and different I was, leaving me feeling alienated and separate from my peers. Every time I didn't get picked for the netball team, or scored low in a test or exam, my *'I'm just not good enough'* belief got hardwired deeper into my subconscious. I spent my childhood feeling and believing that I was hopeless and worthless.

Our perceptions and beliefs are the filter through which we see the world. Just like wearing invisible glasses, our beliefs shape the world we see before us and have the potential to create or to destroy. They either help us move forward in life, or they hold us back.

It's clear to me that it's not always people's lack of action that holds them back, but their lack of self-belief. No matter how much you push, or how hard you try to make things happen, if you truly don't believe in yourself on some level, you will find a way to sabotage yourself. I see it happen time and time again.

I recall one very insightful conversation that I had with my client, Claire. We were talking about the inner guide versus the inner critic. I asked her how she would describe or picture her own inner guide and critic. She thought for a few seconds and then went on to explain how she saw her inner critic as a 7ft tall grim reaper who donned a black cape and towered over her, shadowing every thought or action in her life. She then told me that her inner guide was a three-inch fairy that was fluttering about her head, desperate to be heard over the more dominant tones of her grim reaper. She cried as she realised the enormity of her plight. How was she ever to create the life she wanted with a grim reaper at her throat 24/7? To Claire, it felt like a losing battle.

But here's the thing that you must realise. *You are in control* and you have *free will*. You no longer have to listen to your old programming or your inner critic; you can choose a better thought. You can reconnect with your inner guide, starting right now.

Whatever name you give your inner critic, whether it's Grim Reaper, Saboteur or Wicked Stepmother, it's time to come face-to-face with the voice that has been holding your dreams at arm's length, keeping you in your box and hiding the truth of who you really are. Until you do, you remain powerless.

Understand and accept that you, like everyone else on this planet, have an inner critic or ego. It's just that some people listen to it more than others. Even if this is a new concept for you, it's important to recognise the resistance within you, and the effect it is having on your own happiness. Because when you wake up to this, you become liberated and free.

So, consider these questions:

1) What name would you give your own inner critic? Darth Vader, Lucifer, Maleficent? What feels appropriate to you?
2) What does she/he/it look like or remind you of? Maybe it's a parent figure, an old teacher, a cartoon character, or someone from a movie.
3) What kind of things does your inner critic tell you?
4) In what way have these messages held you back in your life so far?
5) What areas of your life have been most affected? When is your inner critic at her loudest?
6) What is the long-term effect of continuing to listen to your inner critic?

You need to learn how to turn *down* the volume of your inner critic and turn *up* the volume of your inner guide. It really is as simple as consciously remembering that you have a choice. You can listen to the negative messages of your inner critic, or you can listen to the positive voice of your inner guide. *The choice is yours.* Sound easy? Well, in truth, *it is*. We are programmed to listen to the harmful messages we tell ourselves, and it's like a record player going round and round and round.

But we can stop the record, change the music and learn to dance to a new tune!

Start noticing your own internal dialogue, and reject anything that is damaging. Simply say, *"no"*. Some mornings I wake up in a funk and feel down. If I allow myself to stay in this energy for too long, it can literally wreck my day. Instead, I allow myself to look at what's going on and consciously make the decision to tune out and tap in.

My lovely client Louise had been plagued for years by her inner critic and was totally unaware that she could tune out if she wished. She had never really recognised the difference between the two voices until we started working together. And when she woke up to the fact that she could choose who she listened to, the inner guide or the inner critic, big shifts started to happen all around her. She felt much more confident and could look in the mirror without shouting negative abuse at herself. She stopped putting herself down in front of her peers and started to say yes to opportunities. As a result, she changed her career and met the man she came to marry. All this just by just changing her internal dialogue. It's a simple shift in your awareness.

 Today's Assignment:

Start distinguishing the difference between the voices of your inner guide and inner critic. When the inner critic is in full swing simply say, *"I release and let go of this thought, and I hand it over to my inner power right now."*

Day 17 – Open The Channel

Over the past couple of days, I've introduced you to your inner guide and inner critic. This will put the power back into your hands as you choose which voice becomes the guiding force in your life. One will keep you stuck and one will set you free.

But today, I want to take things a little deeper. Because very often, trying to control your thoughts simply *isn't enough*. It's merely scratching the surface. Plus, with thousands of thoughts a day, it's a pretty mammoth task.

When I started learning how to tap into the Divine Infinite Intelligence, I discovered that I could easily manifest some things, and had great trouble manifesting others. I found myself getting frustrated and really questioning whether this whole manifesting thing actually worked. I started reading books on quantum physics and neuroscience, and I came to realise that some of our early programming is so hardwired that trying to change our thoughts just isn't enough. We actually need to change the neural pathways in our brain.

As I mentioned yesterday, children are in a hypnotic state for the first few years of their life and are totally open to being programmed by those around them. They absorb beliefs, ideas and perceptions that are not based on any truth or fact. They are based on someone else's truth. We find ourselves believing we have to work hard for money, that we are unlucky in love, that there's not enough to go around, or that all men cheat. These negative beliefs become the cornerstones of our lives.

As a young girl, my teachers and parents were very concerned that my maths skills weren't up to scratch, and that I was falling behind. I remember overhearing many heated conversations between my parents about my education and feeling like such a failure. I was pulled out of class to have extra help, and I even had tutoring at the weekend. Still, I found maths impossible. My brain struggled to compute numbers. As a result, I formed a very powerful limiting belief early on in my childhood that I just wasn't good enough. This belief wasn't restricted to numbers, it expanded into all areas of my education and I started to doubt my ability to do anything at all. I stopped wanting to get involved in after school activities, I stopped putting my hand up in class, and I stopped wanting to learn. The same thought recurred in my head over and over. What was the point when I was useless? This was my inner critic talking. It was telling me that I was thick, stupid and that everyone knew it. These damaging beliefs were ruining my education and self-esteem. I recall one conversation that my mum had with my teacher at a parents' evening when I was just 11-years-old. It went something like this: *"She's a lovely girl, very kind and willing, but I doubt she'll ever be a high-flyer."* Talk about limiting!

The irony is that I was never ever going to be a maths teacher. My purpose is to write and speak and I hire an accountant and bookkeeper to do my numbers for me! At school, we are expected to be good at everything, but no one can be top of the class in everything they do. We all have gifts and passions and it's these that we should be encouraging our children to develop and pursue.

I left school feeling flawed and incompetent and for the early part of my working life, this *really* limited me. I felt like I was hiding a big secret and that if people found out I had got an F in my maths exam, they would think I was worthless and unemployable. It wasn't until I started my self-development journey that I woke up and smelt the coffee. I wasn't going to let my early programming determine my future. In that moment I changed my life.

Whatever your subconscious mind is programmed with, just remember that these beliefs are NOT based on any truth or fact; they are just your ideas, perception and viewpoint.

Remember this...

'When a limiting belief gets hardwired into your subconscious, your brain looks for evidence in the world to reinforce it. It scans the world looking for supporting confirmation to back up your limiting beliefs.'

Think about this for a second. Reread this statement until it sinks in! Your life becomes a *self-fulfilling prophecy.* You get what you expect to see. Every time I had a maths paper in front of me, my inner critic would tell me that I couldn't do it and I would totally freeze up. If you believe that you're not educated enough, you will look for evidence in life that supports this belief. If you believe all men cheat, you will attract cheaters. If you believe you're crap with money, you will go through your life with a financial leaky bucket. Your beliefs play out as the experiences of your life. Scary, eh?

When I grasped this concept initially, I was dubious. In truth, I didn't want to accept that I'd had a hand in all of the shortcomings and failures in my life. Did I really create those? Surely not! But then I decided that if this crazy concept was true, then surely I had the power to reverse it, surely I could change my beliefs to attract what I wanted instead. So I decided to experiment with my own life.

I didn't tell a soul that I was doing this, but I got straight to work on changing my beliefs and my life. And I've never stopped since. The results are evident to see.

So over the next three days I'm going to show you how to reprogram your mind so that you can *easily* connect with your inner guide and tap into the awesome *Divine Infinite Intelligence* that is waiting in the wings to take you to the promised land.

In order to fully turn down the volume of your inner critic, you need to understand what limiting beliefs are lurking behind its voice. When you can shine a light on your own limiting beliefs, you can change your life and burst through the glass ceiling that you've created for yourself.

Changing your beliefs changes your life and removes the barriers that have stopped you connecting with your inner guide and, ultimately, the Divine Infinite Intelligence.

When you change your beliefs you can co-create anything you want, whether that's more peace, more love, more luck, more money, more faith, more confidence, and so on.

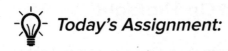 *Today's Assignment:*

You are going to *open your ears* and scan the world in a way that you have never done before. You are going to silently observe everyone that you come into contact with, including your partner, your boss, your hairdresser, the checkout lady in Tesco, the bus driver and your best buddy. Listen to their conversation intently.

Your task is to *listen* to the language they use about themselves.

1) What exactly are they saying?
2) What are the limiting or positive beliefs that underpin what they say?
3) How might this be affecting their lives?

This gives so much away. As you observe, you will start to see the direct correlation between their thoughts and beliefs and the experiences that they are having in their lives. It's profound.

If you have a work colleague who constantly moans about how much she hates her job, notice how this links into her experiences at work. If you have a friend who talks non-stop about her unfaithful lover, again notice how this links into the experiences of her life. How is she creating this for herself? There is always a link between the thought/belief and the actual life experience. *What the mind believes, it receives!*

One word of warning. *Observe in silence.* This is your experiment. Resist the temptation to tell them that their moaning is creating their reality. They won't thank you for it!

Off you go and I'll see tomorrow!

Day 18 – Let's Turn On The Light

Today is a day of *empowerment*. We are going to shine a light on all those *limiting* beliefs that have been sabotaging your success and happiness. Today we are going to set you *free*.

As mentioned already this week, we have a myriad of both positive and negative beliefs programmed into our subconscious mind. Some serve us and some don't. Either way, these beliefs will be producing the outer experiences of our lives. In order to co-create and achieve your goals, we need to make sure that your mindset is ship shape and working for you rather than against you.

No matter what a client's goal is, I always explore their mindset because this will ultimately determine whether they will succeed or fail. And I want them to succeed, and I want you to succeed, too.

While you might put all your effort into achieving your goals, taking action and talking to your inner guide daily, if you have limiting beliefs beneath the surface, you will find that you keep hitting the same brick walls. You will sabotage yourself and keep recreating the same experience in life. This is the *Divine Infinite Intelligence* trying to get your attention. It will keep banging you on the head, over and over again, until you stop being so blind and wake up to the truth. You create your reality!

Here are a few ways that will help you know if you're being blocked by a limiting belief of some kind:

- ➢ You keep attracting the same kind of lover who breaks your heart.
- ➢ You never seem to have enough money, and there are always endless things to pay for.

➢ You never seem to get put up for promotion.

➢ You keep having the same awful bosses.

➢ Your friends never phone you, and when you do speak they always talk about themselves.

➢ You never get asked out on a date.

➢ You never have enough time, and are always rushing around.

➢ You can't seem to get your business off the ground.

➢ You say no to opportunities too often.

After a few years of having my business up and running, things were going really well. I had almost finished my first book, had built a strong mailing list and was effortlessly attracting new clients. I was earning enough money each month and easily sustaining it. I was happy. But I found that I was earning exactly the same amount every month, no matter how many new clients I took on, or how hard I tried. I would pull in the same amount, give or take a few quid. This went on for 18 months until I decided that I obviously had some kind of limiting belief that was creating this financial glass ceiling. Moreover, I realised that my monthly earnings were exactly what I used to earn when I was employed! Clearly, I had a block. So I set about exploring my money mindset.

And what I found was astonishing!

I uncovered a belief that I had adopted from my parents. This was that it was somehow a bad thing to be financially wealthy. My parents didn't like super rich people and were very honest about it. So although I was working my butt off to grow my business and earn more money, my unconscious belief was stopping the increase of financial abundance because I somehow thought that my parents wouldn't like, or even love me, if I was to become rich (whatever 'rich' means). This was quite a light bulb moment for me. I believed, albeit unconsciously, that my parents would reject me if I earned more money. This belief was not good for business and would continue to sabotage me if I didn't do something about it. And, more importantly, it was totally unfounded. Of course my parents would support me, they have always been my biggest fans. They would be over the moon if I earned more money. Uncovering this limiting money belief was a huge turning point, and within six months I had tripled my income. This is the power of changing your limiting beliefs.

Uncovering this belief allowed me to shine a light on it,
rationalise it, and finally make the decision to let
go of it once and for all.

Heather, a client was mine, is a fashion designer. At the age of 38, her big dream was to set up her own studio, create her own designs and sell them to big, high street retailers. But she had spent all of her adult life working for other people, making up their designs and feeling unable to unleash her own creative prowess. She was frustrated. And despite all her best efforts, she wasn't able to make the leap to working for herself. There always seemed to be something getting in her way. Her dream was slipping further and further away and she was losing her passion. We started working together and got clear on her big vision. But before we started to formulate a plan to get her where she wanted to go, we took some time to explore her mindset. I knew this was essential before we progressed any further. When we keep hitting brick walls, it's a clear indication that there's limited thinking at play.

What she uncovered was a big surprise for Heather. She recalled being eight-years-old, sitting in a class and drawing a picture. It was an art project and the whole class was busy working away on their masterpiece. After a while, Heather's teacher walked around the class commenting on the children's work, praising them for their efforts. But when she got to Heather, the teacher became infuriated as she examined her picture. Being a creative spirit, Heather had followed the brief in her own way and created something rather more abstract. She was answering the brief in her own unique way. Her teacher didn't appreciate her alternative take and ripped up the picture in front of her, telling her that it was total rubbish and that she should look at the other children's work and draw something similar. Heather was heartbroken. And in that moment, she decided that it was bad to express her creativity and started looking to her peers for ideas instead. She shut down her inner genius. A belief was formed that it was wrong to be different and express her creative ideas, and that people would laugh and disapprove. This belief was hardwired at the tender age of just eight and carried through into her adult life. *This was the very belief that was sabotaging Heather's career success.* She didn't believe her work was good enough, and thought that everyone else's ideas were far better than hers. This limiting belief was clearly keeping her dreams at arm's length. Consciously she was working towards her dream, but unconsciously attracting something very different. And for the first time in her life, Heather could see this. She decided that she wasn't going to let her, frankly uninspiring teacher, hold her back anymore. It was time to let go of this false belief.

What we believe consciously and unconsciously can be very

different indeed. You might think that you want more money consciously, but are unconsciously telling yourself that you don't deserve it. Or you might consciously tell yourself that you're ready to find Mr. Right, yet unconsciously feel that you'll get hurt again. Remember, it's your deep-seated beliefs that are creating your reality, so you have to go a little deeper than your surface thinking to discover what's really going on.

 Today's Assignment:

You are going to do some brainstorming, but I want you to take a light-hearted approach to it and have some fun.

On blank piece of paper, write down as many of the positive and negative beliefs that you hold about yourself that you can think of. Ask your inner guide to help you with this. Think about the main areas of your life: love, relationships, money, home, work, your life's purpose, fun, health, and so on.

Give yourself time to do this exercise, and let it flow. I want everything out of you head and on to the paper. It might take you a little longer than a day, and that's totally fine.

List everything that you can think of.

Once you have done this, I want you to take a look at all of the negative limiting beliefs that you have listed and underline the three mains ones that you know are holding you back. Remember, we all have hundreds of limiting beliefs, but I want you to focus on the three ones that are stopping you from achieving your dreams.

It's like unraveling a ball of wool; you have to deal with one knot at a time!

Day 19 – What Do You Want To Believe?

Now you've done the hard part of uncovering your limiting beliefs, and you know the score. You've exposed what's standing between you and your dreams. You've switched on the light and it's staring you in the face. What are you going to do about it? Carry on and allow your negative thinking to shape your future? *Or are you ready to make some changes?*

This is probably the most challenging part of this book. It's not always easy to uncover dark beliefs, unpleasant habits and self-sabotaging behaviour, and it's not easy to accept that it has been '*you*' holding yourself back all these years. It's never been about your shitty boss, your cheating fella or your overprotective father. All of your life experiences are simply the result of your past thoughts and beliefs.

But isn't it truly liberating to know that you are no longer in the dark, and you longer have to be held back? You have the power to change your thoughts, and when you master your thoughts, you master your life!

So, before we move on, just take a few minutes to run the following questions through your mind. Write your answers in your journal if that helps.

1) Do you have any idea where these three limiting beliefs came from? A parent, sibling, friend, teacher, etc.?
2) How have these beliefs affected your life so far?
3) What does holding on to these beliefs cost you on a daily, weekly or monthly basis?

4) What will happen if you continue to let these limiting beliefs rule your life?

5) How do you feel now that you have uncovered your limiting beliefs?

It's *vitally* important for you to understand what impact your limiting beliefs are having on your life. Are they stopping you from reaching your full and highest potential? Are they keeping you skint? Are they keeping you in a loveless relationship? Are they creating self-sabotaging behaviour?

Understand what impact your beliefs are having on your happiness, and how they will potentially interfere with your future. Remember, awareness is the key to your freedom. Awareness is your power.

It's time to change your mind!

Are you ready? The first step to rewiring your brain and changing your thoughts is to decide on what you want to rewire it with. What do you want to believe about love, money, your health, your work, and so on?

A question I often ask my clients is: *"What do you need to believe about yourself in order to get what you want?"*

Do you need to believe that there is enough to go around? That you deserve more? That you're capable? Beautiful? Time rich? Can make excellent choices? Have a purpose? Think about what you need to start believing about yourself.

This sounds very simple, I know, but you have to decide from this day forward what your new beliefs are going to be, because they are going to become the foundation of your life. They are going to become the mantra of your day, and help you start co-creating your dreams. They are going to help you let go of all those old beliefs that have been holding your back. They are going to allow the Divine Infinite Intelligence to assist you in your growth and development as a human being.

Your new beliefs are going to be your guiding star. Remember, when you change your thoughts and beliefs you can have *anything* you want in life - anything!

> *When you believe, there is no limitation*
> *on what you can achieve.*

When I uncovered my own money beliefs, I simply decided that I wanted to change my script from *'it's bad to be rich'* to *'it's my birthright to be rich and successful and inspire and motivate others'*. I realised that by being rich and successful, I could help more people. I was actually helping others to wake up and live their life on purpose. This surely had to be a good thing.

The Divine Infinite Intelligence wants to you succeed, and it wants to express itself through you fully in every aspect of life. Everything is programmed to reach its fullest potential. It's only our own limitations within our minds that hold us back from expanding into the best possible version of ourselves.

It's time to change your mind.

It's time to put an end to being held back by your own limited thinking, and it's time to choose a different path - an enlightened one that leads to your freedom.

Think about like this...

'Our beliefs, both good and bad, are like a huge road network in our brain. Our limiting beliefs have been pondered over so often that they become a huge motorway running through the centre of our brain. And because we keep thinking the same negative thoughts over and over again, the motorway gets more and more use, and becomes more and more embedded. Plus, no matter what we do we keep reaching the same dead end. We keep visiting the same destination and recreating the same outcomes in our life. It's a very boring way to live. This is not how it's supposed to be; the Divine Infinite Intelligence wants more for you, and if you're willing to change your mind, it'll show you a brand new road to follow.'

It's time to change your route!

When we create a brand new shiny *'I can do it'* belief, it's like creating a brand new road (or dirt tack) in our brain. Building any new road, or in our case belief (or in technical terms, neural pathway), takes a little time. And like anything in life, you've got to be committed. You have to decide what you want to believe, put down the foundations, lay the tarmac and, most importantly, start taking the new route. And amazingly, the destination is unknown because you haven't travelled this road before. You have no idea where you're going yet, but what you should know is that the destination is going to be awesome!

Enjoy the ride.

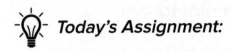 *Today's Assignment:*

You are going to create three shiny new beliefs.

This is a simple process. Take the three limiting beliefs that you uncovered yesterday and reverse them by creating three new beliefs.

Ask yourself: *"What do I need to believe about myself in order to achieve my goal?"*

Some example new beliefs might be...

> ➤ I deserve the best and I accept the best now.
> ➤ Money is flowing freely into my life and I accept it now.
> ➤ My new man is going to walk into my life any day now.
> ➤ I am living my life's purpose.
> ➤ I see new ideas and opportunities every day.
> ➤ Each day I am healthier, stronger and more positive.

Remember, in this process of creating your new beliefs, you are actually generating a new neural pathway in your brain, a brand new road that will lead to *miracle destinations.*

Hop on board and let's start driving.

Day 20 – Reprogramming

Now here's the answer to that all-important question: *"How do I rewire my brain with new thoughts and beliefs?"*

I'm going to be pretty honest with you here. It's down to your commitment and dedication. How much do you want to achieve your goals? How much do you want to find love, discover your purpose, be financially free? It's not enough to know intellectually what your negative beliefs are, and what your new ones should be. *You need to get off your backside and do something about it!*

I didn't want to be stuck working to line someone else's pocket for the rest of my life. I wanted to be free to travel, write, play, experience, and I wanted to leave a legacy for my grandkids. And if that meant working on my mindset to get the things that I wanted, then I was prepared to do whatever it took.

It's a huge turning point in your personal evolution when you uncover the limiting thinking that has been blocking you from reaching your dreams.

We live in a thinking Universe. Those who can master their thoughts and beliefs are the ones who will achieve outstanding results. They are the ones who break records, reach great heights and make historic discoveries. Their clear thinking creates a lucid channel directly to the Divine Infinite Intelligence. Their thoughts and actions literally become Divinely guided.

Today, we are going to formulate *a plan* that I want you to follow to the letter.

I am going to show you how to rewire your brain with your

new beliefs, but you are going to have to commit to this wholeheartedly.

We are creatures of complete habit. We love a good routine, and we love familiarity because we know where we stand and it makes us feel safe and secure. We get up in the morning, we take the same amount of steps to the bathroom and we follow the same routine of going to the toilet, washing our face, brushing our teeth and putting on our makeup, etc. We leave the house at exactly the same time, and we even drive past the same cars on route to work. We repeat the same patterns each and every day. We are habitual by nature. But it's time to mix it up a little. You're not going to like it, in fact, you're probably going to resist it, but if you want to see things change you're going to have to do things differently.

Today I am going to share with you four clear steps and I'd like you to commit to trying ALL of them.

Step 1) Write your three new beliefs down on Post-it notes. Stick them on every surface you can find in your house: your TV, computer screen, kettle, bathroom mirror, car dashboard, knicker drawer, diary, sandwich box, dustbin lid, and inside your saucepans. Don't hold back, get serious about this! If you're worried that your flatmate or hubby will think you've gone all woo woo on them, tell them that you're in the process of reprogramming and to watch this space! Each time you notice your sticky note, you will be sending a new message to your brain. Your brain will pick up on this subliminal signal and embed your new belief further.

You also need to say your new beliefs out loud every day. I used to say mine in the car on my way to work, but you can say them while you are cooking dinner, taking a shower, getting dressed, walking the dog, cutting the grass, etc. There is no excuse. Say them loud, say them clear and know that you are reprogramming your mind with every word you utter.

Step 2) Every night when you are tucked up in bed, before you drop off to sleep, you are going to spend a few minutes imagining yourself living your new beliefs and life. You are going to see yourself having the things you want, doing activities that excite you, and mixing with other people that are on your path. Imagine your life 12 months into the future. See yourself getting into a time machine, and, when you step out of it, you are living your perfect life. Just play this imagining game for a couple of minutes before falling to sleep.

Step 3) Read, study and learn! You need to immerse yourself in self-development work. Always have a book on your bedside table, or an audio on your phone or playing in your car. Throw yourself into this work and you won't fail to rewire your brain. Listen to talks by some of the world's leading thought leaders and gurus. It's your job to feed your spirit and raise your vibrations.

Step 4) Take action! Remember, actions are the engine to your dreams. Action is quite simply the fastest way to rewire your brain with any new belief system. With each new action step you take, you start to believe in yourself more and more. And before you know it, you are achieving things beyond your wildest dreams.

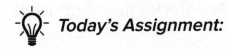 *Today's Assignment:*

Try all of the steps listed and commit to your plan.

When you commit to making these four simple steps part of your daily routine, you'll quickly start to notice changes occurring. You'll start to feel stronger and more confident. But most importantly, you will notice that the blocks that were previously there have withered away. As a result, you'll start manifesting everything you need effortlessly into your path to achieve your goal.

Day 21 – Your Day For Reflection And Rest

Take time today to let what you have learned this week sink in.

Also, take a couple of minutes to answer the following questions:

1) What *insights* have you gained about yourself this week?
2) What have you *discovered* about yourself that you weren't aware of before?
3) How are you *feeling* about what you have learned?
4) How might this *change* your life for the better?
5) What is the most *important* thing that you must now do?

Prayer for this week:

"Dear Divine Guidance, please show me all that is holding me back from living the life I desire. I am willing to let go of all limiting beliefs, patterns and habits that would lead me to sabotage my own happiness. Thank you for helping me to adopt new positive thoughts and beliefs that will serve me on my journey to living a rich and abundant life. Help me to know that I am perfect as I am and that I deserve good now."

And so it is.

WEEK 4

DAYS 22-28

Mastering Your Practice

Days 22-28

Mastering Your Practice

Many of us, although desperate for something to change in our lives, are not really prepared to do things differently. We start off with good intentions only to give up when things get tough.

Life is tremendously busy for all of us, and very often our outer world seems far more real than our inner one. As a result, the physical part of our life wins our attention most of the time. We want *immediate* results and *instant* gratification. We want to set a goal one day and see a result the next. Many of my clients will try a technique for a few days only to come back and say that it didn't work. Of course it didn't work! If we're inconsistent, the results we receive will be inconsistent. If we truly want to change things we have to hook up and *stay* hooked up. It's that simple. We wouldn't go to the gym twice and expect it to transform our body, so why would we expect anything different when it comes to exercising our mind and spirit?

Every autumn, as the weather starts to change, the children and me plant spring bulbs: daffodils (my favourite flower), tulips, crocuses, hyacinths and fritillarias. The kids bury the bulbs deep into the fresh soil then pat the soil down and water them, leaving them in a sunny part of the garden to mature over the long winter months. The bulbs are totally forgotten about until the spring, then one beautiful bright morning we wake up to find that the first hyacinths have popped up through the soil. For months we see neither sight nor sound of the flowers making an appearance, yet we have total faith that they will emerge. Why wouldn't they? Why would we doubt nature? We cannot set our goals one day and expect them to come to fruition the next. We cannot meditate for a few days and expect to feel dramatically transformed.

We are spiritually lazy. We get bored, we get tired, we forget, we get lost in others people's dramas, we have chores to do, work projects to complete, dinner to cook and washing to put on. Our outer world seems *far more important* and real so our inner world gets neglected. Yet this problem is our undoing.

Being an all or nothing kind of gal, I give things my full commitment. I believe that this is why I have experienced such profound results in my life. I know that everything that I share with my clients works, and I know this because I've seen it work for myself.

When we really start to focus on balancing all four elements of ourselves consistently - mental, physical, spiritual and emotional - our lives will transform.

There have been many occasions in my life when I've got so lost in my mental side, over thinking things and planning for the future, that I've forgotten to nurture my spiritual and emotional side. As a result, I disconnect and I switch off my power. So as you work on fulfilling your blueprint, your values and your gifts, and as you begin focusing on your goals and taking action, you must not neglect your inner self.

This week I'm going to show you how to nurture your inner world and create a powerful daily practice that is going to keep you totally connected and on track towards your dreams. You'll be able to fit this around your lifestyle, no matter how busy you are. I'm also going to explain why it is important to create your energy vortex, and why meditation, visualisation and prayer should all be part of your daily routine.

Let's get started!

Here's a brief rundown of what I'll be getting you to do this week:

Day 22

I'll be showing you how to create a *special place* within your home. This is your personal energy vortex and you will retreat to it daily to rebalance and energise your spirit.

Day 23

We'll look at how you start your day, because if it begins the right way, *the rest will flow with ease.*

Day 24

I'm talking *meditation*. Why it's fundamental to your health and how you can easily make it part of your routine with little effort.

Day 25

This is my favourite day of this entire book. I'll be sharing with you the most *powerful co-creation* technique that I have discovered.

Day 26

I'll be showing you how you can have your inner guide on speed dial at all times.

Day 27

You are going to map out a daily practice that fits in perfectly with your busy life.

Day 28

Your time for reflection and rest.

Day 22 – Creating Your Space

Today you are going to have fun creating your own personal *energy vortex*. You are going to construct a space in your home that is yours, and yours alone. This is a place that you can retreat to daily to connect with you inner guide. Here you should be free to meditate, pray, visualise, read a book, listen to music, sing, dance, or whatever else feeds your spirit.

Let me tell you why it is so important to do this...

'If your house is anything like mine, it can be really hard to find a quiet five minutes for yourself. Our homes are often a hub of activity, whether that's because of children, housemates, partners, pets, or even electrical appliances: TV, phones, computers, and so on. They are all emitting energy. And this affects our energy. The energy in your kitchen is probably very different to the energy in your bedroom. Well, at least I hope it is!'

Having a space that you can call your own allows you to take some daily time out. And when you keep coming back to the same place, an energy vortex forms around it. Constructing your space should be about creating a peaceful, harmonious and still energy that you can bathe yourself in every day. When we meditate, pray, sing, or dance in the same location, we create a lovely high vibration. And the more times we return to that spot, the higher the vibration gets. Plus, you'll notice that you'll be able to relax far quicker in your familiar spot than if you move to a new location each time.

Have you ever noticed the vibration of a church? Hundreds of years of service has created a frequency of serenity that we can undoubtedly feel as we enter one. And this is the energy that I want you to create in your home, or, more realistically, in a particular corner of your home.

You might be wondering about where on earth you will find the space. But I'm not necessarily talking about having a whole room to yourself here. Think along the lines of a chair in your bedroom, a corner of your office, a large pillow that you put on the floor, your bed or a quiet corner of the garden.

One of my clients uses her dressing table. Another bought a small Buddha water feature for a secluded part of her garden and uses this as her space. I have a lovely comfy chair in my office that no one other than me tends to sit on. This is my space. It's where I go to when I need five minutes to myself. My chair has magic powers, honestly!

So think about your own home and where the best place is for creating your energy vortex. Remember, you are going to keep coming back to this space over and over, so it shouldn't be too much of an effort to create it. You don't really want to be hauling furniture around each time you want to meditate. Keep it simple. It doesn't have to be fancy; it just has to be somewhere that you'll be happy to retreat to each day.

Where will your space be? Ask your inner guide to help you find the right spot in your home.

Once you have decided where your space will be, you need to think about what you'd like to fill it with. Think about bringing to it a special cushion, a soft luxurious blanket, scented candles, a vase of your favourite flowers, a frame with a special photo inside, ornaments, a religious statue, a sentimental piece of music, an important book, your journal, joss sticks, angel cards, crystals, or anything else that makes you feel at ease and relaxed. Remember, it's your space.

It's also a great idea to create an altar. I use a little coffee table next to my chair and place a few special items on it that I like to have next to me when I meditate. I have my favourite Doreen Virtue tarot cards, a beautiful pink salt lamp, a few special ornaments, an amethyst crystal that I hold when I meditate, some meditation beads, my dream board, and a little black and white photo of my mum and me. I like to have all of these special things next to me when I take time out, whether I'm meditating, praying, visualising or doing something else - they make me feel connected and at peace. I always find it easier to relax when I'm in my special space with my items around me.

If an altar isn't appropriate for you, think about creating a happy box. Buy yourself a pretty box, or simply decorate an old shoebox, and fill it with special things. Each time you sit down in your chosen space bring out your happy box. One of my clients even puts chocolate in hers.

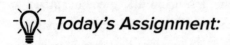 *Today's Assignment:*

Today's task is really easy. Decide on where your chosen space will be in your home.

Set the intention that this is now your space. It's your own personal energy vortex that you will retreat to when you need time out, or are working on co-creating your future. Ensure that your space is inviting and that you'll want to keep visiting. Create an altar or make up a happy box and have fun doing it. If anyone asks about what you are doing be truthful and tell them that this is your personal space for relaxing and taking time out. Encourage them to create their own.

Most importantly, make sure that you visit your space every day. The more you visit, the higher the vibration will be and the more powerful your energy vortex will become. It will literally become a power spot within your home. *How cool is that?*

Day 23 – Good Morning World!

I recall a while back hearing the queen of self-help herself, Louise Hay, say: *"How you start your day is how you live your day, and how you live your day is the way you live your life."*

Pretty profound, eh!

I'm definitely a night owl and have always found it difficult to wake up early. I love my bed way too much. And in all honesty, you wouldn't want to be anywhere near my house at 7am in the morning. My house is a cacophony of noise as I round up the kids for school. I'm normally frantically searching for a missing school tie, or screaming at the kids to finish their Weetabix. You can imagine! I'd love to tell you that I do some kind of lovely relaxing meditation before I start my day, but I'd be lying.

My clients often ask me about my daily practice and what I do to keep myself in good shape, both inside and out, especially as I have two children and a business.

Despite my manic morning routine of getting the kids off to school, I do have a daily practice that is non negotiable and fundamental to me living a peaceful and fulfilling life. In fact, my daily practice has changed my life. I encourage all of my clients to adopt a daily routine which involves them taking time for themselves. I'm going to be telling you about creating your own daily personal practice on day 27.

But today I want to talk to you about your morning routine, and how you start your day. Whether you're a night owl like me, or a morning lark like my 5-year-old son (6am bright and early every morning, without fail), it's important that you start your day in a positive and effective way.

Have you ever noticed that when you wake up grumpy, the crotchetiness tends to snowball as your day progresses? What starts off as a simple moan about the weather can leave you feeling like the world is against you by the time you go to bed.

Our thoughts and feelings create our experiences, and in order to have an awesome day, it's vital we keep our vibes high. The higher our vibration, the more miracles will come our way and the better our day will be.

Now, before I continue, let's get something clear.

'We need to get real for a second. We are human and born to experience the whole array of emotions that we're born with. Happy versus sad. Fear versus peace. Good versus bad, and so on. We're here to experience the lot, and where would the fun be if we only experienced one end of the spectrum? Some days you will wake up in a funk. You will break the heel on your best shoes, you'll miss the train or you'll argue with your man. This is called being human. This is normal. We cannot avoid all negative emotions. What we can do is become aware of when our vibrations are dropping. From this place we can create miracles. This is because we can change our thoughts and actions to something more positive, something that will elevate our vibrations back to their natural state of wellbeing.'

My job is to teach through my books, articles, courses and private work, but I too have shitty days, and I am human just like you. But when I find myself in a funk I dig deep into my toolbox to raise my vibrations instantly. I don't stay down for very long, and this is the key.

What I've come to learn is this: how I start my day has a massive impact on the kind of day I have. When I take time in the morning to mentally, physically and spiritually prepare for my day ahead, I have a better one. It's that simple.

When you start your day setting the intention that it's going be awesome, and when you connect with your inner guide and the Divine Infinite Intelligence, you will undoubtedly have a day filled with heavenly miracles. It's like switching on a light.

It doesn't make sense that you would start your day any other way!

So how do I start my day? As I briefly explained, my house is rather crazy in the mornings, but I do still make time to ensure that I am starting my day off on the right foot. Like everyone else, my routine is pretty mundane. I wash, dress, put on my face, do my hair, get my kids ready, prepare breakfast, drink a green smoothie, make lunches, maybe put a wash on, make the beds, round up the kids and all their paraphernalia, and then we're off out the door to school. It's a pretty speedy and stressful start to the day.

But here is when my morning practice comes in. Come 9.15am, I'm back from the school run and ready to start my day. Before I log on to my computer, check my mail or eat breakfast, I take five minutes to set my intention for the day ahead. I play a favourite piece of music and I do a few basic energy routines, which involve clearing my chakras, grounding myself and repeating a mantra for the day. I then say a prayer for the day ahead; this can vary greatly depending on what is going on in my life. All in all it takes me no longer than 10 minutes each morning.

Once it's complete, I feel mentally, physically and spiritually ready for what the day has to bring.

This is my personal morning practice and it won't necessarily work for everyone. You need to find your own morning routine. This could take the form of a morning run, some journaling, or you might like to start your day with a meditation in your energy vortex or by listening to an audio in your car. But what's important is that you take a couple of minutes *each* morning, whether that's 6am or 10am, to set your intentions for the day ahead. Most importantly, *keep it simple*. Don't set yourself up to fail by creating some over complicated routine that you're going to find hard to stick to.

Another important point I'd like to share with you is that we often set ourselves up to fail by trying to be perfect. If you miss a day, so what! Just carry on the next day. At weekends, my normal morning practice goes out the window and that's OK. My routine is very different at the weekend. I like to have a lie in and lounge around in my PJs. Cut yourself some slack and be *gentle* on yourself. Yes, consistency is important, but missing a day or so really won't hurt.

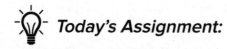 *Today's Assignment:*

Create your morning practice.

*Remember, how you start your day is how you live your day,
and how you live your day is how you live your life.*

What new simple habits are you going to create for yourself
starting from tomorrow? Plan out *exactly* what that looks like and
exactly what you're going to do, whether that's pray, meditate,
exercise, work on programming your new beliefs, journal, sing,
dance, do some yoga, and so on.

Put reminders around your bedroom or kitchen so that you
don't forget. Do this for a week or so and it'll soon become a habit.
I guarantee that if you commit to a morning practice where you
set your intentions for the day, you will start to notice profound
results.

Try it and see.

Day 24 – Tuning In

Today, I want to talk about tuning in and turning *up* the volume with the Divine Infinite Intelligence. Research has suggested that the key to attaining the things we want in life, whether that's abundance, career success, health, happiness or enlightenment, lies in a particular state of mind. And I couldn't agree more.

For hundreds of years, meditation was an exclusively spiritual practice for serious seekers. Yet as we move through this exciting time in our evolution, meditation is becoming more and more commonplace. Everyone seems to be at it! By quieting the mind and deeply relaxing the body, the person meditating experiences deep states of inner peace and, ultimately, higher states of consciousness. It's been found to have significant benefits for people with a range of health conditions, such as heart disease, high cholesterol levels, high blood pressure, insomnia, chronic pain, and cancer. There are countless benefits to this wonderful practice.

But many people wrongly believe that meditating is about sitting quietly for hours on end thinking about nothing. This is not the case. Meditating is about quieting the mind in order to go inwards in search of greater self-awareness. It's an active training of the mind to *increase your awareness* of self and your union with the Divine Infinite Intelligence.

I call it tuning in.

Here's what I know to be true about meditating:

'The more you take time to meditate, the more content you feel with life. No matter what is going on around you, you will feel at peace.

But what's really exciting is that when you slow your thoughts down through meditation or mindfulness, you open the channel to the Divine Infinite Intelligence. You connect with that power within. You receive Divine guidance and great ideas come to you. You find solutions to your problems, and get clear on the steps that you need to take in order to move your life forward. Everything you need is given to you when you open the channel and connect.'

Meditation strengthens your sixth sense and gives you access to your inner power, and that's life changing.

I found meditation purely by accident. I was going through a huge transition at work and found myself reading self-development books to help me through it. One of the books I was reading had a chapter about meditation, which I found fascinating. I was intrigued enough to try it for myself. And the very first time I sat down to meditate, I had an overwhelming experience that I still find very hard to explain to this day.

I was simply repeating the mantra suggested: *"I am love, I love and I am loved"*, over in my mind with no expectation whatsoever. But within a couple of seconds of repeating the mantra, what can only be described as a surge of energy entered my body through the top of my head and quickly moved through my body and chest. It was incredibly powerful, like a force hitting my body. I can only liken it to a drug-induced euphoric state of being. I started to panic as this unexplained energy overtook my body and, in that moment, the sensation disappeared as quickly as it came. I was left feeling really disorientated and shaken; I had never experienced anything like that before and couldn't rationally explain it away.

From that moment on, my life was never quite the same again. And I have never experienced anything quite so powerful since.

In that life-changing moment, I was woken up by the Divine. I was given a clear message that we are so much more than our physical bodies; we are spiritual beings, living in a physical body and here to play the game of life. I became very aware that I had work to do on this planet and that it was time for me to upgrade my life and find a new direction.

And a new life is exactly what the Divine Infinite Intelligence helped me to create. Meditation became a way of life, and it opened the channel to Divine guidance. Slowly but surely, I changed my life.

The Divine Infinite Intelligence is calling on us all to live bigger and better lives. This is our birthright and is very much ours for the taking, whether that's a career shift, finding love, restoring our health or increasing our financial abundance. The Divine Infinite Intelligence can help you, and meditation is a clear channel for you to receive the guidance you need. Remember not to be scared when you meditate. You are not going anywhere, so there is no need to fear. Meditating is not a form of mediumship. All you are going to do is quiet your mind and open the channel. You are going inward in search of self-awareness. And in my experience, insights, ideas and solutions don't often come while meditating, they pop into your mind when cooking dinner, taking a shower or walking the dog. But the more the channel is open, the more information you'll receive. *It really is life-changing stuff!*

Meditation is an important practice for me in my life, but like everything, I don't put too much pressure on myself. If I get time to do it daily then great, if I don't then that's okay too. But what I do notice is that when I neglect my practice for too long, I feel disconnected. It's as if the channel slowly closes off. Intuitively I know when it's time to retreat to my space and put on my meditation music.

Not only is it a daily practice for me, but I also do it when I have a bad day, or I feel low in my mood. I turn to meditation rather than a glass of wine. I would much rather drown my sorrows with my inner guide than with a glass of chardonnay.

So, whether you're completely new to meditation, or already practising it, I'd really like to encourage you to up your game. The truth is that if we are inconsistent with our spiritual practice, the results we get will appear to be inconsistent, too. The more we commit, the more we will get out. But remember, when I say commit, I'm not talking hours and hours a day - I'm talking minutes a day. We have to make it fit around our lives. We still have to eat, wash, sleep, work, shop, play and exercise, so make your meditation practice work for you.

Here are my suggestions for getting started:

> *Create your sanctuary*

Where is best for you to relax where you are not likely to be disturbed? Is it in your spare room, the garden, the dining room, in the bath? Decide where is best and stick to the same location each time you meditate. Yesterday we talked about creating your personal energy vortex, and this is a perfect place in which to meditate.

> *Use whatever you have to help you relax*

You might like to consider lighting a candle while you meditate, or having a special ornament, photo or vase of flowers next to you. Anything that will make you feel more at ease and relaxed.

> ➤ *Decide on your posture*

There are many different meditation postures, from the most commonly known lotus position, a cross-legged position with the feet resting on the opposite thighs, to the very simple position of sitting on a meditation cushion. You need to do a little research and find what works for you. Personally, I don't use any prescribed position. I just sit on my favourite chair with a blanket wrapped around me.

> ➤ *Do not be disturbed*

There is nothing more frustrating than being interrupted while you're in a deep relaxation. So switch off the phone, lock the door and ensure that you're not likely to be bothered. Before I meditate, I make sure that the kids are fast asleep and that everything is turned off.

> ➤ *Write down any insights or thoughts*

Consider keeping a journal of your experiences, or any insights that you have. This is great to refer back to.

> ➤ *Be guided by a voice*

While learning to meditate, you might find it useful to record your own voice, which you can then use as a guided meditation. Or try buying a guided meditation CD to follow until you feel comfortable doing it on your own.

> *Set a timer*

It's a really good idea to set a timer for three, five or 10 minutes, or even listen to a particular piece of music. That way you will have a start and an end to your meditation rather than sitting there wondering how long it's been. You'll be amazed at how quickly a 10-minute meditation flies by.

Mini meditations

Rather than meditating once a day for 10 minutes, how about doing mini one-minute meditations throughout your day? When I was working in full-time employment, I would often nip to the ladies for a quiet mini meditation.

Remember, meditation is tuning in. *It's your connection to the Divine.*

 *Today's Assignment:*

I'd like you to decide how you're going to make your meditation work for you.

Do you prefer the idea of mini meditations throughout your day? Is a morning meditation more preferable to an evening one? Where are you going to meditate? Are you going to listen to music or a guided meditation audio?

Starting today, find just a few minutes to meditate. The aim is to make this a new daily practice for *going forward.*

Day 25 – Co-Creation Station

As I stated earlier, day 25 is my favourite day of this 40-day programme. Why? Because what I'm about to share with you has undoubtedly revolutionised my *entire life*, and I'm utterly passionate about imparting this message to the world.

We live in a thinking Universe. Everything in our world started with a single thought. Your house was once a thought in an architect's mind, the pen you use was once an idea in a designer's mind, as was the car you drive, the shoes you wear and the wallpaper on your wall. Everything started as a small seed in someone's imagination.

We are co-creators and we are here to create what we want using our thoughts. Remember, your thoughts are the engine to your dreams.

Passionate thought turns into real action, and action eventually manifests as physical matter. We bring things into being using our imagination. This is how the world works.

Wallace D. Wattles, an American author of 'The Science of Getting Rich' said: *"Man can form things in his thoughts and by impressing his thoughts upon formless substance can cause the thing he thinks about to be created."*

The Divine Infinite Intelligence responds to passionate thought. We co-create with the Divine. This is what we are here to do; this is playing the game of life.

But here's the stark, cold truth:

'Most people don't realise that they have this internal power to co-create and therefore don't allow themselves to dream, or, even worse, they imagine the worst-case scenarios.'

Your thoughts are the field where everything is created:
good, bad or indifferent.

I intuitively knew this from a very early age. I loved using my imagination (like most kids do) and was often lost in my own little fantasy world. As I grew, the world took hold of me and I adopted countless limiting beliefs and restrictive perceptions about myself and how the world worked. But I never lost the ability to daydream. When I wanted something badly enough, such as the latest Levis 501s, my first Peugeot 205, my first office job, a sexy boyfriend to wine and dine me, I would fantasise about how it would feel to have these things in my life, even though I hadn't got them yet. I found it fun to daydream. It was escapism for me. But what I didn't realise at the time was that I was co-creating. The Divine Infinite Intelligence responded to my call and I pretty much manifested exactly what I wanted as a result. I've manifested some pretty shitty things too in my time, but that's a conversation for another day! On the whole, I was pretty damn good at getting what I wanted. But at the time, I just thought I was very lucky somehow. I'd look around me and see that others didn't appear to be quite as lucky as me

In my early 20s, I remember a work colleague commenting snidely that what Louise wanted, Louise got. I remember feeling hurt because I was being perceived as some kind of spoiled brat who has had everything handed to her on a plate. But this couldn't have been further from the truth. Everything I had in my life, I had created and worked hard for. I had simply taken the opportunities that had come my way.

It wasn't until a few years later that I discovered the truth behind this so-called luck.

Why is it that some people have all the love, luck and abundance while others have nothing? We're living in a thinking Universe; it is a law of nature that began at the start of time. What we think we become. I have always been good at channelling my energy towards the things I want and, as a result, I get them!

Visualisation fires up new neural pathways in our brains. It literally rewires them and creates brand new belief systems.

When I was able to understand what I had been unconsciously doing, I started to consciously put my energy into creating a more purposeful direction for my life. I began to visualise what I wanted to do with it, and I asked deeper questions about my calling. I focused my energy on attracting more abundance into my life, and yes, you guessed it, things started to change very quickly. Exciting and scary opportunities came my way as my old life started to fall away. The Divine Infinite Intelligence was responding to my new call.

Believe me, it wasn't always easy. I was thrown a few curveballs to contend with, and I had to let go of many things that no longer served me. But it was certainly worth it. Invariably, when we start to co-create new things, we have to let go of the old. As the new world emerges the old one must be released, and this can be downright painful.

But, what I really want you to hear is: *"It's worth it!"*

It's time to start harnessing the power of your imagination

Use it to help you reprogram your mind and bring your goals to fruition.

Visualisation is used by some of the world's most successful people, including authors, entrepreneurs and athletes. Almost every athlete plays the race in their mind before the event. They go over the muscles that they will use, how each one will tense and how much power they will put into each jump or sprint. Every successful person will tell you the same thing. They could see their success long before it happened.

> *Don't underestimate the power of your mind – science is only*
> *just discovering the influence that our minds have*
> *on the world around us.*

Just a few minutes of creative visualisation a day can change your life in unimaginable ways. It's just that most people *don't* believe in their own imagination.

Not only does visualising communicate to the Divine, it also rewires your mind so that you can attract and manifest what you need in order to make your dreams a reality.

Here are a few things for you to consider before you give this a go:

Repetition is the key to any new skill. Just like meditation, you need to commit in order to see the outer results in your life. But again, we're talking about only a few minutes here. The best time to visualise is either first thing in the morning when you're still in bed, just before you're about to fall asleep, or in the shower or bath. We do these things every day so you should find integrating visualisation into your practice really easy.

While visualising, imagine that you are looking through your own physical eyes. See things as you would in the real world and make your picture as bright and as bold as you possibly can.

Put emotions into your dreams. We create through passionate thoughts, not wishy washy ones. Feel the passion as you visualise. Imagine how it would feel to achieve your goal, whether that is to secure your dream job, meet your perfect partner, become a mother, buy your first home or travel the world.

While you are visualising, don't let any negative thoughts get in. Imagine shutting your inner critic outside the door, so that you are in peace with just your inner guide.

 Today's Assignment:

You are going to take five minutes to sit in your energy vortex and pretend that you are the movie director of a film about your life.

You have complete say about what happens in your movie. Nothing bad can happen because you are telling the story.

Now *direct* your chosen movie. Play out in your imagination the life that you would like to be living once you have achieved the goals you outlined in week two.

1) Where do you wake up?
2) What is the weather like?
3) Describe the people you share your life with?
4) How do you behave around each other?
5) What are you wearing/how do you look?
6) How do you spend your days?
7) How do you spend your evenings?
8) How are you feeling?

Remember, we live in a thinking Universe; your thoughts create your future.

I'd like to encourage you to make visualisation part of your practice, whether you take time to sit in your energy vortex each day, or whether, like me, you do it whenever you get the opportunity, in the shower, while ironing, or before you go to sleep each night.

Just a few minutes of creative visualisation a day can change your life in *unimaginable ways.*

Day 26 – Dialing Up

I have always said prayers. As a child, my mum would tuck me in with a nighttime prayer. We'd pray for family members, starving children and the sick and lonely. Sometimes we'd repeat the *Lord's Prayer* together, too. And occasionally, I'd pray for a new Care Bear or My Little Pony. It was a very comforting ritual, which was as much a part of my life and routine as brushing my teeth.

My Catholic mum went to a convent school in Ireland in the early 60s, along with her nine brothers and sisters. She was taught to fear the wrath of God and was sent off to Mass every Sunday morning along with her siblings. Each child in turn would go into the confession box and repent for their sins that week, which could be anything from sticking their tongue out at their superiors to not eating all their dinner. They would then be told to pray to a particular saint depending on what they were repenting for. It was all very serious and very much fear-based. One tale I remember my mum relaying to me took place when she was just six-years-old. All of the children in her family (and there were lots) were forbidden to eat their breakfast on Sunday mornings until they had come home from Mass. On one particular Sunday morning, my mother was very hungry and decided that she couldn't wait until after church. She pinched a sausage from the kitchen counter that had been left to cool, gobbled it up in secret and instantly felt awful at her wrong doing. She never told a soul, apart from the priest who ordered her to do ten Hail Marys to ask forgiveness for her dreadful sin. For her, prayer was about repenting in fear. She worried that if she didn't she would be stuck in limbo when her time came to pass.

So prayer passed down from my mother was very much a daily obligation, even though I wasn't brought up Catholic or taken to church often. Before I'd go to sleep, Mum would ask, *"Have you said your prayers, Louise?"* She certainly never ever encouraged me to repent for any of my sins (it would have been a very long prayer indeed), but simply helped me form a dialogue with something greater than myself. And I thank her so much for opening my mind to this and helping me form this practice; it helped me to create a bond with the Divine from a very young age. I truly felt that someone somewhere was hearing my plea.

As I progressed on my spiritual path, I started to learn more about prayer and its true purpose in my life. For me, prayer is no longer a duty or something I think I should do; it's more like dialling up to have a chat with my inner guide or the Divine Infinite Intelligence. It's a connection to that *greater part of myself.*

If meditation is about heightening your awareness and receiving guidance, then prayer is like a telephone line to heaven. It's an opportunity to commune with the Divine.

Sometimes life can be very lonely, especially as we traverse the spiritual path. As you develop and learn more about yourself, it can really feel like those around you just don't 'get' you anymore. It's very hard to share your innermost thoughts with people that don't really understand you.

When you pray, you no longer feel lonely, and there is a subtle shift in your energy field that you will be able to feel. So whether you're used to praying as part of your own religious or spiritual practice, or whether this idea is very alien to you, I really want to encourage you to dial up to heaven more often. It offers so much support and comfort - not just in times of need, but each and every day.

Most people only drop to their hands and knees in times of need, as if the Divine only answers our call when we're desperate. But *why wait* until you're at your wits' end before asking for assistance? Doesn't it make sense to ask for help each and every day? You can tap into the Divine Infinite Intelligence at any time. In fact, the Divine doesn't want you to wait until the shit hits the fan before you dial up, it's more than happy to have you on speed dial so that you can call as much as you like.

Think of it as like having an imaginary friend (aka your inner guide). Just like with any friend, you can tell her anything. What you're excited about, what you're terrified about, how you're feeling and what your deepest desires are.

I pray in the morning as part of my daily practice, and again at the end of the day. I always start my prayer by saying thank you for whatever has been happening in my life, however big or small. I send love to my family members and then, depending on how I'm feeling, I might ask for help with my emotions or a particular task that I need to accomplish. There is certainly nothing formal about the way I pray: it's just a conversation with an old friend.

Praying, like meditation, visualisation, and many of the other techniques I've mentioned, raises our vibrations. It lifts us higher, and from this elevated position comes a wonderful sense of peace and tranquility.

I'd like to offer up a few suggested prayers for you to try out. But why not make up your own? After all, they are some of the best prayers of all. If you're uncomfortable with the word prayer simply substitute it with something else like *'contemplate', 'dial up'* or *'converse'.*

Suggested prayers:

Dear Inner Guide,
I am willing to release the blocks that keep me from receiving your gifts. Thank you for helping me to raise my own vibration so that I may attract Divine miracles into my life.

Dear Inner Guide,
Thank you for helping me to shine my light today so that I may inspire others. Show me where I need to go, what action I need to take and who I need to speak to for my own personal development and happiness.

Dear Inner Guide,
Please guide all my thinking and actions today.

Dear Inner Guide,
Thank you for helping me to see the good in my life and feel the emotions of peace and gratitude as I go through my day.

Dear Inner Guide,
I know in truth that you are bigger than my earthly problems so thank you for guiding my thinking and my actions today. Thank you for sending me a miracle!

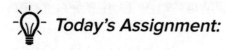 *Today's Assignment:*

Start praying.

Dial up and start having a chat with your inner guide. Play with this idea. Explore and investigate it, and then *give it a go!*

I have created a pretty little prayer book, which I keep next to my meditation chair. Inside, I have noted down favourite prayers that I have heard over the years and made my own. I have a prayer for peace of mind, for increased money, for improving relationships with my loved ones, for health, for business, and so on. I find this a real comfort. Maybe you can create your own prayer book, too?

Day 27 – Your Daily Practice

If you are serious about changing your life for the better, then you have to get *serious* about looking after your mind and spirit. They are just as important as your physical body. And when we take care of ourselves on all levels: spiritually, emotionally, mentally and physically, that's when our life changes for the better.

This is where we have been going so wrong. You can't just take care of one part of yourself, it doesn't work like that. If you're too focused on the mental, your emotional and spiritual side suffer. And if you're too caught up in the spiritual, the physical can get neglected. It's time for you to nurture your *whole self.*

Having a daily practice in place will really help you to keep in balance on all levels.

This is what I know for sure.

'When I make time for my daily practice my day is blessed in unimaginable ways. Things just seem easier and I feel more connected and peaceful. When I skip my practice, I feel stressed. Ideas don't flow as readily, and I feel tired and unmotivated.'

Having a *daily practice* keeps your connection to the Divine alive and kicking.

So what is a daily practice? It's simply a series of small things you do for yourself each day. This could be exercise, meditation, relaxation, self-hypnosis, prayer, mantras, art, journaling, affirmations, yoga, dance, walking the dog - anything that makes you feel good and gets you connected to the Divine. When we're connected we are truly at our best and life flows effortlessly.

As I mentioned on day 23, every day, once the kids are dropped off at school, I take five minutes to play some music, do some energy exercises and set my intention for the day with a little prayer. I finish my day when the kids are tucked up in bed with a short meditation and closing prayer. This practice is my life-saver and I wouldn't be without it.

> *Making a little time to get balanced each day can have a tremendous effect on your life. Don't take my word for it, try it and see for yourself.*

Ask yourself what your daily practice should consist of? What makes your heart sing? What relaxes you and makes you feel connected to something greater than yourself? When is the best time of day for you to practise? Are you a lark or a night owl? Is the morning time perfect for you, or does mid-morning suit you better?

And finally, ask yourself *how are you going to make this a habit*? Good intentions so often get pushed to the back burner. So how are you going to integrate this new habit into your day? Maybe you need to set a reminder on your mobile, or set your alarm so you get up five minutes earlier in the morning.

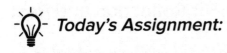 *Today's Assignment:*

You're going to master your daily practice.

I want you to take everything you've learned this week and form your own personal daily practice. Write it down on a little note as a reminder to yourself. Remember, you're creating a new habit, so you're going to have to give it a little time to embed. It won't take long and you'll quickly start to feel the benefits.

Your routine might look something like this:

Example:
Morning
Listen to visalisation/relaxation audio on phone while on train to work. Plus five minutes of stretching/dog walking.

Lunchtime
Take a walk in nature on lunch break. Read or listen to an inspiring/thought provoking audio book.

Evening
10-minute mediation/visualisation followed my some journaling and prayer work.

Day 28 – Your Day For Reflection and Rest

Take time today to let what you have learned this week sink in.

Also take a couple of minutes to answer the following questions:

1) What *insights* have you gained about yourself this week?
2) What have you *discovered* about yourself that you weren't aware of before?
3) How are you *feeling* about what you have learned?
4) How might this *change* your life for the better?
5) What is the most *important* thing that you must now do?

Prayer for this week:

"Dear Divine Guidance, thank you for helping me to find peace and quiet within my home so that I might find the time and space to connect within. I ask for increased faith and willpower at this time as I establish my own personal practice. Thank you for clearly showing me that I do have an unearthly support team that I can call upon at any time."

And so it is.

WEEK 5

DAYS 29-36

Mastering Your Vibes

Days 29-35

Mastering Your Vibes

Every person and object we see around us is made up of energy. Our pets, home, favourite pot plant, car, the food in our fridge… they are all a living, vibrating mass of Divine energy particles. Put simply, energy is at the very core of our being and forms the building blocks of our entire Universe. *Everything* is a string of complex energy information.

Our entire body is a mass of subtle energies moving in and out of form. Each of us is a delicate pulsation of intelligent power that resonates with the energies of everything around us. If you were to look at a blade of grass, or your kitchen work surface, or a piece of your skin under the most powerful microscope, you would see swirling particles of mass within that substance.

Everything in life, including air, water, earth, rocks, trees, animals and humans, consists of particles of energy, and each is vibrating at a different speed. We are literally living in the most mind-blowing energy matrix you could possibly imagine.

For example, you use your Wi-Fi connection every day at home. You know that you are hooked up to the World Wide Web even though there are no visible wires that directly connect you. You are composed of energy just like those invisible Wi-Fi currents running through your house. If you touch a live wire you definitely know about it. You feel the energy. So many things in life that exist are invisible. Just because you cannot see the energy doesn't mean that it isn't there.

Have you ever stopped to ponder the magnificence of life? Have you ever thought about the force within you that has the power to make your heart beat, your blood flow, your cells regenerate, and new life to be created through you? This life-force energy has such power that all these things happen effortlessly and without your intervention. This immense power makes life possible everywhere. Trees blossom every spring, snow falls every winter and the sun rises every morning. But what is this power and where does it come from?

Deep down, we all feel this power under our feet. We feel the connection, the union and the authority, however subtle. Yet most of us have become so detached from it that we've literally lost our way. Our vision has become distorted by superficial things such as what car we drive, how much money we make and what handbag we're carrying. We are all looking for instant gratification. We've got caught up in this outer superficial world that is based on materialism, power, greed and fear.

Now let me get one thing straight. I am a girl who likes her Estée Lauder makeup. I adore an afternoon spent shopping and I get great satisfaction from organising and colour-coding my wardrobe. I like my material luxuries, and I'm not about to give them up anytime soon. And I'm certainly not about to retreat to some faraway mountain top and hum mantras all day long!

But what I have realised is this:

'In order to feel truly 'rich' in life, we need more than the material world can offer us. We need more than pricey mascara and a fleeting two-week holiday in the sun each year. We need more than our new car, our iPad, or a box of Thorntons. It simply isn't enough to contain our spirit. This is because we are more than the material world. Within us is something so magical, so powerful and so all-consuming that when we wake up to the truth about it, life is never quite the same again!'

It's wake up time. And wake up we must if we want to live a purposeful, meaningful and fulfilling life. Living a disconnected life is challenging, exhausting and very painful at times. A disconnected life lacks meaning and purpose; it feels like there is a void that no matter what you do, or how much you own, remains unfulfilled. We try and fill this void with food, sex, clothes, money, but none of these things work for very long. And the sad thing is, so many people go through their whole life feeling this emptiness inside.

There is a whole new reality waiting for you to step into. And once you open the door, your life will never be the same.

The Divine is constantly tapping us on the shoulder trying to get our attention and show us the truth.

Each and every one of us is energy, and we are all born connected. It's just that somewhere along the way we've forgotten this truth.

The return back to your real authentic self isn't always straightforward. It takes courage, determination and *real* commitment. Waking up from a life of limiting habits and beliefs is challenging, but also truly liberating. You will no longer be held back and will be free to spread your wings, fly and explore new lands. Your journey will be unique for you, and everyone must travel at a speed that is right for them. It's an organic process that we can't rush. Like a baby, it arrives when it's good and ready.

I am so passionate about deepening my understanding of how life works. It's a subject that captivates me. I have an eagerness to discover more and more; it's like a burning fire of desire within me that I have to keep fuelling.

Education and knowledge is paramount to our personal freedom. This is what will change our world. Yet our understanding is totally back to front. When we start to take care of our energy bodies alongside our physical bodies, our lives will quickly transform before our eyes. As we vibrate at a high frequency, we start scanning the world in a totally new and profound way, and we attract amazing things into our sphere. We literally become magnets for good. Our bodies feel healthier, we are more vital and, most importantly, we feel more contented.

Yet most of us ignore our body's subtle energies and pop pills to ease physical or emotional pain. We look to a broken old archetypal system for answers, and end up going round in circles as a result.

It's time to enter a new paradigm.

This week, I'm taking you a little deeper into the realm of energy. This is about *deepening your understanding* and getting to know your energy body. As a result, you will naturally raise your own vibration and change your life and the lives of those around you.

Here's a brief rundown of what I'll be getting you to do this week:

Day 29

I'll be introducing you to your *bio-field*, also known as your *auric field*. I'll be explaining its importance to your wellbeing and, most importantly, how you can strengthen and protect your aura from negative energies.

Day 30

We'll be talking *chakras*, those portals of swirling energy located deep within the human body. Your body is a conduit for energy to flow through, and your chakras move vital life-force energy through your body to ensure vitality. When your chakras aren't working efficiently, they can't push through sufficient energy and you feel totally out of balance. I'll be showing you how to cleanse and clear your own chakras.

Day 31

Is all about *meridians* - the energy bloodstream. The meridians carry life-force energy. No energy means no life-force! So I'm going to show you how you can use your own energy system to determine how food, drugs, toxins and thoughts directly affect your body.

Day 32

We're going to switch on your vibes and become aware of *energy vampires!* I'm going to show you how to protect yourself from other people's energy, and also how to build your intuitive muscle.

Day 33

It's time to focus on finding your *flow*. When we live in the flow, life is magnificent because it naturally raises our vibrations and attracts more good into our lives.

Day 34

I'm going to teach you *four energy exercises* that have made a significant difference to my life. Use these daily and you will keep energy flowing freely around your body, helping you to feel more alive and connected.

Day 35

Our day for rest and reflection.

Day 29 – Strengthening Your Own Energy Field

I am sure you've heard of the word *'aura'* before. Your aura, or *'auric field'*, is a multi-layered shell of energy that surrounds your physical body. The material it is made up of is less dense than your physical body, and it vibrates at a faster speed. It's a protective atmosphere that surrounds you, filtering out bad energies and drawing in the ones you need most. The aura has been studied since 500 BC, and it has been scientifically proven to exist. Science refers to it as your *bio-field*, and by using special equipment you can measure, see, feel and even photograph it.

The aura is a vibratory field that surrounds all living things, and even inanimate objects. This is because everything is made of energy particles, so it naturally follows that everything has an energy field around it. Your auric field vibrates much faster than your physical body, and this is why the human eye doesn't often detect it. Some people are able to perceive the faster vibrating particles of energy in the auric field and they describe them in varying colours. For example, we all associate the colour red with anger and the colour green with envy. Your auric field literally turns red when you are angry and green when you are jealous of someone.

Contained within your auric field is what are known as *'subtle bodies'*. These are often referred to as your *emotional body, mental body* and *spiritual body*. Each subtle body layer vibrates faster than the physical body and increases in speed the further away it is from the body. Similar to a CD disc, the auric field records deep life experiences and stores it in the vibration that makes up the subtle body material. Everything you feel, think and do gives off an energy that comes through in different colours, shapes and shades. *The aura is your spiritual blueprint.*

Along with your five physical senses, your auric field and subtle bodies are designed to help you perceive and sense things for the brain to compute. Your aura is literally an antenna sensing the world around you. It gives you so much information about what is and isn't good for you.

Have you ever walked into a room and felt a negative vibe in the air? Or met someone new and instantly disliked him or her? How did you perceive this instantaneous information? It is your energy field bringing you higher frequency messages from the world around you, just like an insect detecting a predator. Yet most of us have shut down this sixth sense and are ignoring the subtle messages that our bodies are giving us. Our body never works against us and is constantly trying to communicate with us.

There are many characteristics that make up the aura. Everyone's aura is unique. But if your energy frequency resonates with someone else there will be great rapport, and you will hit it off like a house on fire. You will feel an energy connection.

However, if the frequency differs, it is likely that there will be an initial dislike for the person, or you will feel like they are almost keeping you out, as if they have an electric fence around them.

Your energy field is *always interacting* with everything around you. If you interact with lots of people every day it can really affect your aura and leave you feeling drained and wiped out. We have all experienced this. I find it very hard to be in public places for too long because I'm like a sponge picking up everyone else's thoughts and feelings. I also find it hard being around people with lower frequencies.

Fortunately, nature is a great cleanser and literally cleans and balances your aura of anything negative. In some cultures people swam in the sea when they got sick. I think we can all agree that a walk in nature or a stroll by the sea feels wonderful, and we always come back feeling better than when we left.

What I find really cool is that a group's energy is always greater than an individual's. *Collectively* our energy is much more powerful. So the more contact you have with a group of people, the more your own frequency changes. Before long, you will start resonating at the same frequency as the rest of the group. This is brilliant if it's a high vibrational group of people, but not so brilliant if it's not.

When your aura is weak you are much more vulnerable to what I call '*energy vampires*' (I'll be talking more about this on day 32). We unknowingly allow people to steel our positive energy and this is why we sometimes feel drained when we've been with a particular person. I know that when I'm feeling down, frustrated, cross, stressed out or agitated it affects the behaviour of my children, and they start playing up and being naughty. My energy morphs with theirs and we all end up feeling grumpy! As the old adage goes, '*When mummy's happy, everyone's happy!*'

Some other things that can weaken your aura are; poor diet, lack of exercise, lack of sleep, stress, drugs, prescribed meditations, alcohol, environmental pollution and negative thoughts and beliefs. All of these things affect your auric field greatly.

One area that particularly interests me is food. There are so many nasty additives in our food these days, and they have a direct impact on our energy system. They lower our frequency, cloud our thinking, reduce our mood and make it very difficult for us to connect with the Divine Infinite Intelligence.

When you consume whole foods that are grown organically, which have high life force energy, they charge your own vibrational field with positive energy.

The fact of the matter is this:

'If your energetic field is weak you can become like a sponge for disruptive energy, and this will take its toll on your physical body. When your mood is low, your aura literally crashes inwards, forming a shield around you that isolates you from the rest of the world. When this happens you feel helpless, lonely and don't want to talk to anyone. Conversely, when you are feeling alive and happy, your aura can fill the entire room.'

Think about when you're listening to someone talk on stage and are totally captivated by him or her. Their aura is reaching out and embracing you - and you can feel it!

Most of us have lost our innate ability to see auras.
However, we can still feel energy.
It's just a matter of sharpening up our gift.

I feel people's energy all the time - it has always been my gift. I don't even need to be in the same room as someone else in order to sense how they are feeling. I can talk to someone on the phone and pick up on their emotions. And I can walk past a stranger in the street and detect their thoughts and feelings. I'm not unique. Everyone can do this with a little awareness and practice.

Occasionally I can see someone's aura, too. I remember the first time I actually saw someone's auric field. I was sitting in my office talking to one of my colleagues across the room. As she was talking, I saw a blue hue appear around the top half of her body. I blinked a few times, but there was no mistaking the sea-coloured field of energy surrounding her body. As I started to doubt myself, it disappeared as quickly as it had come.

There are many ways that you can strengthen your own energy field, and I'm going to be sharing lots of these this coming week. You can try alternative energy therapies to restore balance, but as a coach I'm passionate about empowering people to take charge of their own wellbeing by creating a daily practice that they can do at home. I'm going to share two techniques for you to try, which will help protect your own energy field.

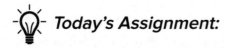 *Today's Assignment:*

Expanding your aura

You can do this anywhere, but you get extra benefit from it by doing it in nature. If you live in a big city, do it by a window. Start by standing flat on your feet, knees bent and palms resting on the top of your thighs. Take a deep breath. Now, bending at the waist, use your hands to literally scoop the energy towards your body. Do this by rolling your hands over each other as you raise them from the floor to above your head. Once your hands are above your head, shimmy the energy over your back and down your sides, as if you are taking the energy you just scooped up and helping it to cascade down your body. Your hands should remain about six to 12 inches from your body. With time, you will be able to feel your auric field and your intuition will guide your hands.

You can do this for a friend, too. Simply use the same process as above, but this time use your hands to scoop the energy towards their body rather than yours.

Fluffing your aura

Stand flat on your feet with your knees bent and palms resting on the top of your thighs. Take a deep breath. Put your hands above your head, keeping them six to 12 inches away from your body. Now work your hands down your body, making fluffing motions as if you're patting the outline of a cloud. You will be able to feel the energy, it's like a soft cloud or cotton wool and it has a bounce to it.

Once you tap into your energy and your intuition, you will be able to feel where the auric field ends. This is where you should do the fluffing. Don't get caught up in questioning whether or not you are doing the exercise right - you can do no harm and it will still be helpful to the aura if you get it a bit wrong. You can do this for a friend as well. Simply use the same process as above but use your hands to make the fluffing motion around her or his body. To see a demonstration of this, please visit www.gameoflife.co.uk/latest-book/

Day 30 – Your Energy Portals

To further understand your energy system, I want to introduce you to your *charkas*, aka your *energy portals*.

The word chakra translates from Sanskrit as disc, vortex or wheel. Chakras are portals of swirling energy located deep within the human body. They start at the base of the spine and finish at the top of your head.

You have seven major chakra points (energy centres also known as *chi* or *prana*). *These are:* the *root chakra*, the *sacral chakra*, the *solar plexus*, the *heart chakra*, the *throat chakra*, the *brow chakra* and the *crown chakra*.

Each chakra supplies energy to specific organs and corresponds to distinct aspects of your personality.

Your body is a conduit for energy to flow through, and your chakras move vital life-force energy through your body to ensure vitality. The chakras in the lower part of your body spin more slowly and relate to issues of the material world. The chakras in the upper part of your body spin faster and correspond to more spiritual issues. I tend to think of chakras as a spinning ceiling fan, which is rotating clockwise.

Different chakras are influenced by your thinking; so the things that you tend to focus on most, such as money, relationships, your work, and so on, affect your energy centres. If you hold negative thoughts, your chakras become clogged up and dirty. When your chakras aren't working efficiently, they can't push through sufficient energy, leaving you feeling totally out of balance. When your chakras are spinning freely and smoothly, your life flows the same and you'll find yourself experiencing harmony and bliss in your daily life.

Your chakras also affect your intuition and your connection to the Divine Infinite Intelligence. With cleansed and balanced chakras you'll be able to connect with the Divine with greater ease.

Each chakra is designed to bring you different information about yourself and the world around you. And each one is a warehouse of information about who you are. Think of each chakra as a disc of information similar to the hard drive of your computer. For example, your first chakra hard drive would be imprinted with information about your physical body, your connection to the physical world and your security. The second chakra hard drive contains information about your creativity, your emotions and your relationships. Conversely, the crown chakra tells you about your connection to the Divine Infinite Intelligence.

Each chakra hard drive is a precious source of data about you, including your past, present and future. Tapping into this warehouse of information is one of the *greatest* sources of self-discovery available to you on your spiritual journey.

Every event, relationship, issue and painful moment of your life is computed through your chakra system. Unexpressed or unrecognised feelings, thoughts, judgments and truths can back up energetically and cause congestion and blockages within the chakra system. This causes all manner of problems from physical disease and emotional stress, to self-critical damage. It's important to understand what each chakra represents and what we can do to keep this energy flowing freely.

Muladhara - The Root Chakra

This is located at the *base of the spine* near the tailbone area. It relates to stability, grounding, money and physical needs.

Svadisthana - The Sacral Chakra

This is located near the *lower abdomen*, about two inches below the navel. It relates to sexuality, balance, emotions, physical grace and pleasure.

Manipura - The Solar Plexus Chakra

This is located near the *upper abdomen*. It relates to vitality, power, direction, self-esteem and self-will.

Anahata - The Heart Chakra

This is located in the *centre of the chest*, just above heart. It relates to love, compassion and altruism.

Visuddha - The Throat Chakra

This is located in the *throat*. It relates to communication, resonance, creativity, speaking your truth and authenticity.

Anja - The Brow Chakra

This is located at the *forehead* between the eyes. It relates to intuition, perception, imagination and wisdom.

Sahasrara - The Crown Chakra

This is located at the very *top of your head*. It relates to spirituality, intelligence, awareness, universal source and oneness.

As part of our daily or weekly practice, it's vitally important to keep our chakras cleansed and clear. Every day we take a physical shower to wash away the dirt of the day.

> *Clearing and cleansing your chakras is like taking an emotional shower, and it should be done daily.*

 ## Today's Assignment:

Cleansing and balancing your chakras.

Try these steps to ensure that your chakras are clear and balanced. It's one to practice daily.

Step 1) Take a few moments to relax and focus on the rhythm of your breath.

Step 2) Visualise your root chakra at the base of your spine. It's a beautiful, bright red ball of spinning light. Notice if your chakra is dirty or clogged in any way. Trust what you're seeing. Your body does not lie.

Step 3) Now visualise cleaning your chakra, maybe with a feather duster, or maybe using a vacuum to suck away all the unwanted negative energy. Clean your chakra thoroughly until it's sparkling clean. Now see your chakra totally balanced. It's spinning brightly and freely as it should.

Step 4) Repeat this process for each of the other chakra points: the sacral chakra (orange), the solar plexus (yellow like the sun), the heart chakra (emerald green), the throat chakra (sky blue), the brow chakra (indigo) and finally the crown chakra (violet). Visualise the colour of each chakra and notice any areas of darkness or dimness that need clearing away.

Step 5) When you have cleaned each and every chakra, step back and visualise all of your energy centres sparkling brightly and spinning freely and smoothly.

Step 6) Surround yourself in a big ball of protective white light. When you're ready, bring your attention back to your surroundings.

If you're struggling to visualise cleaning your chakras, try holding your hand just above each chakra point and keep it there for a few minutes, moving your hand in a clockwise direction.

Day 31 – Your Energy Bloodstream

While chakras supply vital energy to specific locations, *meridians* move energy all over our bodies. They transport energy in the same way our veins transport blood. In short, our meridians carry life-force energy. No energy, no life-force!

Donna Eden has been teaching people how to work with the body's energy systems for over 35 years.

She writes in her book *Energy Medicine:* *'The meridians affect every organ and every physiological system, including the immune, nervous, endocrine, respiratory, digestive, skeletal, muscular and lymphatic system. Each system is fed by at least one meridian. If a meridian's energy system is obstructed or unregulated, the system it feeds is jeopardised. Your meridian pathways also connect hundreds of tiny electromagnetically distinct points along the surface of the skin. These are known as acupuncture points and can be stimulated with needles and physical pressure to release or redistribute energy along the meridian pathway.'*

As well as keeping our chakras clean and spinning freely, it's also important that our meridians are able to distribute vital life force energy around our bodies. We are conduits for energy to flow through, and it's so important that we keep it flowing. This maintains our health both physically and emotionally.

Let me tell you a little story about how I really got in touch with my own energy system...

For years I suffered with my skin. From my early 20s, I was

plagued by a skin condition on my face. I would develop unsightly and itchy lumps that would last for weeks on end. Doctors thought that it was a condition called rosacea, but I wasn't convinced. The treatment they prescribed didn't help much. I found myself reliant on antihistamines and antibiotics to alleviate the symptoms. Anyone who knows me will tell you that I don't pop pills lightly. So this didn't sit easy with me.

This went on for *years,* and I went round in circles trying to figure out what it was that was causing the distressing lumps on my face. Was it stress? The hard water supply in our area? My diet? My makeup? I played about with my diet endlessly trying to find the culprit for my troublesome skin. I spent hundreds of pounds experimenting with new makeup, but all to no avail. I simply couldn't get to the bottom of it and was at my wits' ends.

It was really knocking my confidence, and when I was suffering with a particularly bad attack, I didn't even want to leave the house. Anyone who has suffered with a skin condition knows how this feels.

I prayed for Divine guidance to show me the reason for my bad skin. And the answer came in the most unusual way.

I discovered energy testing. This came about through researching facial acupuncture, which I'd been told was super at aiding skin conditions like mine. As I was doing my research and looking for a local acupuncturist, I became fascinated by how energy flows around our meridian system and affects our wellbeing. As I got deeper into the subject, I discovered energy testing - and this is where my life turned a huge corner.

There's no better way to really get to know your energy field, inside and out, than to energy test yourself. If you want to find out what your energy field responds best to, what compromises your energy and functioning and what subconscious thoughts/beliefs/memories sabotage your ability to grow and change, energy self-testing is key.

For me, it was the first time in my life that I was able to start communicating with my own body. And I was bowled over by what I discovered.

Energy testing involves testing the body's responses when applying slight pressure to a large muscle. This provides information on energy blockages, the functioning of the organs, nutritional deficiencies and food sensitivities, among other things. In a typical example of muscle testing, you are given a herb or a particular food to hold in one hand and are asked to extend your other, keeping it straight. The practitioner then presses down on this arm and your opposite shoulder with equal pressure (to ensure balance). If the herb or food is something you need, you'll be able to resist the downward pressure and hold your arm rigid. If not your arm will easily drop. You can hold your straight arm pointing forwards or sideways, depending on which meridian you want to test. Either way, it's a great way to communicate with your own body.

So imagine the scene.

One Sunday evening, I excitedly laid out on my kitchen work surface every food I could think of: eggs, milk, chocolate, wine, meat, yoghurts, tea, sweets, vegetables, fruits, and so on. By the side of these, I spread out the entire contents of my makeup bag and all the other self-care products from my bathroom cupboard.

I then instructed my husband to muscle test me on all the things that I had laid out. I showed him how it worked and got him to blindfold me so that there would be no mental influence. In turn, I held a bowl containing each food item, followed by all my self-care products. With each item, my husband made a note of what remained strong and what weakened my energy field.

Guess what the culprit was for more than a decade of skin-related distress?

Sugar and additives. It wasn't dairy or wheat, or even my makeup as I'd previously thought. It was SUGAR! My body can't tolerate excessive amounts of sugar, or any kind of food additive. It literally freaks out when either of these things hits my system. My body had been shouting at me for years, but I wasn't listening. We were talking different languages.

But interestingly, I also noticed that stress and negative thoughts dramatically affect my energy system. When I brought a negative thought to mind, my energy system would weaken in the same way it did with sugar.

I had my answer. Stress and sugar were the cause of my skin troubles. Finally I was able to understand what my body needed. I was euphoric.

In her book, *Energy Medicine,* **Donna Eden says:** *'If I had the power to impact the medical profession in just one way, it would be that physicians add energy testing to their diagnostic tool kit.'*

Like a fingerprint, each person has a unique energy system. The foods we eat, the supplements we take, and the thoughts we think impact each of us differently. Our body resonates with certain vibrations and tenses against others, either stabilising or stressing our system. What better way to find out what is good for your body than to test it for yourself?

What really fascinates me about energy testing is how negative thoughts impact on our energy system, just like foods do. When you hold a positive thought in your head and test your muscle strength you remain strong, yet when you think of a negative thought you immediately lose your muscle strength. This is how fast your thoughts affect your physical body.

Maybe you have been putting up with a health problem, too. You could be experiencing symptoms but are unclear about what is causing them. Maybe you just want to know what effect your limiting beliefs are having on your body and test out how your new beliefs can impact your system. There is so much you can do with this.

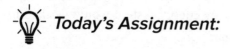 *Today's Assignment:*

You are going to get a friend/partner/colleague to muscle test you.

To begin, stand with your feet no more than shoulder width apart. Place the substance you are testing in one hand and close your fist over it. Hold this hand up to your heart centre and hold your other arm straight out to the side. Your friend is then going to test the strength of your arm. If you can easily resist the pressure of your friend pushing down, then your body is okay with the substance you're holding. If your arm goes weak under the pressure, it's a clear sign that your body doesn't like it. It really is as simple as that.

It doesn't necessarily have to be a food substance. Remember, you can try out your new beliefs with this, too.

For a visual demonstration on muscle testing simply visit www.gameoflife.co.uk/latest-book/

Have fun!

Day 32 – Trusting Your Vibes

It's time to start *trusting* your vibrations. Remember, your energy system is like an antenna and it's there to serve you – so start using it.

On the morning of the Boxing Day Tsunami in 2004, many of the animals inhabiting the coastline that was about to be struck ran for higher ground, leaving us humans to take the full force of the wave. We didn't see it, or - more to the point - *'feel'* it coming. Nature and animals can feel vibrations, but we have shut down this innate ability and it's time for us to reclaim it.

In order for you to trust your vibes you must absolutely *'get'* that you are psychic and have the ability to tune into the larger energy fields all around you. Even if your psychic ability is lying dormant right now, know that it is there. Tuning into energy fields is totally normal and very much a part of being human.

I have always felt energy. As a child I could tell when my mum was unhappy, I could pick up on how my teacher was feeling when I walked into my classroom and I always knew when a friend was lying to me. In fact, it is impossible to tell me a fib and get away with it. I have a very strong internal lie detector. I know when my kids aren't telling the truth, I know when a client hasn't done their homework, and I know when a friend cancels a meet-up and isn't truthful about her reason. Put simply, I feel it in their energy. As a result, I find it extremely hard to lie myself.

We've all had the experience of feeling that someone isn't being honest with us. When you felt it, you were most probably right! Yet so often we ignore the *'hunch'* and end up in all sorts of horrible situations that we could have easily avoided had we only trusted our vibes.

To get started on this path to higher living, you must first accept that you are indeed intuitive, even if it doesn't feel like it yet. You just need to tone up your intuitive psychic muscle.

How often have you thought of a friend just before they called or sent a text? This is no coincidence; it's simply energy we're picking up on. One reason many of us find if difficult to tune into our vibes is *exhaustion*, both physical and emotional. Exhaustion is like death to our vibes. Sleep deprivation, stress, unhealthy foods, medications and pollution all lower our frequency so much that we can't tap into our intuitive vibes. When you're tired, you literally become a slave to your inner critic. You disconnect and everything feels so much worse. This is because you cannot think or feel when you're tired and burnt-out.

It's often said that a good cry and a good night's sleep solves everything, and there is so much truth in this. Remember, when you sleep, so does your mind chatter (inner critic) and this allows you to reconnect with your intuitive voice within (inner guide).

Sleep allows your energy system to reboot, your emotions to rest and the Divine connection within to wake up. This is why everything feels better in the morning.

Rest is just part of the equation; food is another. Eating pure whole foods will naturally sharpen your ability to feel your vibes and become more open and intuitive. As I explained yesterday, sugar and me don't get on very well. Reducing my sugar intake has had a massive impact on my intuitive ability. As soon as I reduced the sugar in my diet, my frequency shot up. I could think more clearly, I received clearer messages from my inner guide and my energy levels were super high. Living in a higher way isn't about living exclusively on a raw diet; it's OK to have the odd piece of cake from time to time because that's the fun of being human, but we cannot expect to eat junk and then receive clear Divine guidance. It doesn't work that way. Pure body equals pure thoughts. Sugary sweets, endless cups of tea or coffee, ready meals and alcohol will not help you. But hey, you know this stuff already. I'm just here to remind you! The cleaner your food intake, the higher your vibes will rise. The higher your vibes, the greater the miracles that you will be capable of manifesting will be.

One thing I know for sure is that when we *don't* take care of our physical bodies and neglect ourselves, we switch off our vibes and cannot hear our inner guide. Our meridians stop flowing efficiently, our aura closes in around us, our chakras get clogged up and we become energetically toxic. And nobody wants to be in the presence of someone who is toxic. When energy doesn't flow as it should, the Divine can't be heard and we become disconnected. Your body cannot live in corrupted energy.

When you allow Divine energy to flow through your body, you become an energy magnet. You become alive and shine brightly. And who doesn't want to be in the presence of someone who is shining?!

Our energy field is very delicate and it doesn't take much to throw it off balance. But the price we pay for disconnecting and losing our intuitive ability is the feeling of being lost, confused, directionless, frustrated and depressed. Living your life with your vibes switched off isn't how it's meant to be.

Before I take action on decisions or opportunities, I check with my vibes first. This is because I've learned the hard way that when I ignore my vibes, life gets bumpy. It's almost as if I derail. When I stay connected to my vibes and my inner guide, I always make the right decision, which brings me joy and abundance. This is not to say that I never make a wrong decision. I am only human! But I only ever make the wrong choices in life when I'm overwhelmed, stressed out, tired, or have been neglecting my body. When I allow my inner critic to run the shop, life goes a bit tits-up. Luckily, I'm much more aware nowadays and am able to turn things around pretty quickly and get back on track. And this is what I want for you.

The most effective way to switch on your vibes or clear toxic energy is to get outside and connect with your body and the ground at your feet. This will get your energy flowing again, clear your mind and get you focused.

Also, remember your energy vortex from *Week Four, Day 22* - the place you retreat to daily to bathe yourself in peaceful energy? This is a great place to tune into your vibes when you become disconnected. You'll find that when you commit to your daily practice, you'll be far more tuned into your vibes as you go about your day-to-day life. The more you commit to your practice, the more intuitive you'll become. You'll start using your natural antenna, sussing people out and making decisions that are Divinely guided.

It's *very important* to point out that while you can work on raising your own vibrations, you are also picking up energy from those around you, whether this is at home, work, on the train or bus, or in the shopping aisle at Tesco, and so on. We exchange energy with everyone we interact with. Have you ever chatted with someone only to be left feeling totally drained afterwards? Or have you experienced the opposite, when you've left a conversation feeling so much lighter and happier? This is because you are either giving away your energy or receiving it from someone else.

It's important to watch out for what I call *energy vampires*. Energy vampires suck you dry leaving you feeling wiped out. If your vibes are naturally high, people will unconsciously be attracted to your vibrant energy and they'll want some of it! This is why it's so important to regularly spend time in your energy vortex, as it rebalances your energy field. Also, expanding or fluffing your aura, as we discussed on day 29, is very important as it keeps your energy field strong and protected.

The act of taking energy from someone else, or having them take energy from us, is called energy hooking. These are simply energy exchanges. It's vitally important for us to ensure that we haven't got any leaks in our energy field. So today I'm going to show you how to protect yourself, and how to build your intuitive muscle.

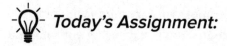 *Today's Assignment:*

There are three things that I want you to try in order to heighten your vibrational awareness.

1) Keep your energy flowing daily by getting outside and spending time in your energy vortex. This naturally cleanses and clears your energy. Also, protect yourself with the aura exercise we spoke about on day 29.

2) At the end of every day, ask yourself if anyone that you've interacted with is still connected to your energy field. This could be your boss, partner, kids or a friend. Your body will let you know if you have any energy vampires sucking at your life-force. Imagine an energetic cord stretching from you to them, or vice versa. Now imagine simply cutting that cord so you are released from one another.

Please note: what you are doing is not a bad thing. You are not cutting them out of your life; you are simply preventing them from taking your energy. Releasing someone who is feeding off your energy actually gives them their power back because it encourages them to go within themselves to discover what they need. Of course, they might also go in search of another victim! Either way, you must protect your own energy field.

My son has a very strong energy field, and is a hugely intuitive little boy. But he also sucks on my energy field all the time. This is what children do. So at the start and end of every day, I show him how to clear his own energy field. And before I go to sleep, I cut the cord that connects us. This way I get my energy back and so does he. It serves us both and makes us stronger.

3) And finally, set the intention to notice your vibes as you go about your day-to-day life. How do you feel when you walk into a particular setting? Can you feel a shift in the atmosphere? How about when you're with your partner, child, or friend? Can you pick up on how they are feeling? Tune into your sixth sense and it will change the way you live your life.

Day 33 – Living In The Flow

When we live in the flow, life is magnificent. When our life-force is flowing we are 100% present and living life as we should.

Wayne Dyer an internationally bestselling author calls it, *'Living your joy.'*

These are moments in life in which we are totally absorbed by what we are doing and lose all sense of time. Flow can be described as a narrowing of focus, a sense of being engrossed, and a feeling of transcendence and *being present.*

Any activity can lead to flow: playing a game, listening to music, walking the dog, cooking, writing a blog post, playing, creating, and so on - but it must be an activity that you love.

> *When we spend more time in the flow,*
> *life really is a joy to live.*

But here's the problem...

'We don't live in the flow very often. In fact, we don't really know how to live in the flow nowadays. Most days we find ourselves incessantly striving for a clean loo, disinfected worktops, a clear inbox, a flatter tummy, school gate acceptance and career success. We've got too much on our plates, and we're always focused on what's next, leaving no time for the things that bring us joy and make us flow.'

We live life at breakneck speed; we are constantly connected to technology, we have stressful working lives and hectic home lives.

We are overcommitted, burnt-out and trying to be everything to everyone.

Finding your flow is really about simplifying your life and slowing down.

But first off we have to discover what *makes* us flow. What activities bring us a deep sense of inner fulfilment and pleasure? I'm always talking to my clients about self-care and having more fun.

We are on this planet to *play* for goodness sake; we're here to experience all that we can, and we can't do that by working day in, day out. Yes, we have to pay our bills, do the washing and walk the dog. These things will always need our attention and they're not about to disappear anytime soon. But let me tell you this. You're not going to look back at your life when you are 90 and wish you had loaded more washing into the machine or spent more time organising your paperwork. Come on! All these things are irrelevant in the grand scheme of things. Ask anyone who is nearing the end of his or her life.

What you are going to wish you had done more of is the exciting and fulfilling things like playing snakes and ladders with your kids, painting pictures, talking to your mum, eating cake, climbing trees, swimming in the sea, dancing and having sex.

The priceless moments that stand out for me are sitting on a windy British beach eating homemade sandwiches while watching my children play, laughing around the kitchen table with friends, being totally lost in writing an article or a chapter for a book. In these moments, I'm most definitely in the flow of life. My energy is flowing and I feel connected to something very powerful.

One question we may all ask ourselves at the end of our life is: *"Did I live fully and did my life matter?"*

I am terrified that when I get to the end of my time on Earth, I will have regrets about what I missed.

This is my motivator to live my life to the full. You will always regret the things that you didn't do, but you'll never regret the things you did.

> *We all need more flow in our lives,*
> *because when we flow we let the Divine in;*
> *we're in tune with our vibes and it feels awesome.*

This isn't about relinquishing all our responsibilities. We still have to meet our commitments and ensure that we get our needs, and the needs of our families, met. I still have to tackle my pile of ironing every week, do my grocery shopping and clean my house. These things are my responsibility. But I am very aware that I must also make time for moments of joy in my life.

Children instinctively know how to flow. They naturally seek out the experiences and activities that will allow them to be in the moment. It's only as we get older that life can bog us down, causing us to forget how to flow or to get our needs met in unhealthy ways.

I worked with one client a few years ago who came to me stressed out, lost and disconnected. We spent time working out her core life values and getting clear on the things that made her flow. It transpired that music was her thing. She loved the joyful sounds of Latin music and spent a lot of her childhood listening to her parents' records. There was something about the beats and melodies that made her heart sing and made her feel alive. I asked her to recall the last time she listened to Latin music, and she couldn't. So we decided we'd try a little experiment. Each evening when she arrived home from work, instead of busying herself with chores, she played some loud Latin tunes in her flat. Sometimes she just sat down and listened, other days she'd dance around the living room. When we got back together a few weeks later she shared what a significant difference it was having on her mood. For the rest of the evening she had more energy and motivation. Shortly after reconnecting with her music she decided to take up Latin classes in her local community hall and subsequently met her soul mate!

Remember, when energy is flowing we are connected to the Divine, and miracles happen when we are connected to the Divine.

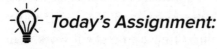 ## Today's Assignment:

I want you to brainstorm 25 things that put you in a state of flow.

These can include music, cooking, dancing, people watching, sewing, exercising, gardening and performing. If you come up with more than 25, even better. Do not stop until you have 25 or more.

Now pin your brainstorm someplace where you're going to see it regularly. Your aim is to find your flow each and every day, even if that's just stroking your cat or reading a good novel. The more you flow, the higher your vibes and the more connected you are.

Day 34 – Your Reset Button

Everyone on this planet is on an evolutionary journey to learn, grow and expand. Some people resist growth and others embrace it.

I continually want to grow and expand. I cannot help it! My soul and spirit feel fed when I'm learning and experiencing new things. We're either in the process of sowing seeds in life, or we're harvesting our crop. We are either learning or putting into practice what we've learned. But when we're not doing any of these things, our life-force energy diminishes and our spirit starts to scream out.

Personal growth is a constant cycle of learning new things, and it's a cycle that has served me tremendously well. I am an all or nothing type of gal. Anyone who knows me will tell you this. I am an extremely ambitious and determined soul. If I decide to try something new, I give everything I have to make it work. Full commitment is important to me, as I hate to do things half-assed. What I know for sure is this. When we are inconsistent with the Universe, the Universe is inconsistent with us. It's that simple. We must apply ourselves fully if we are to really change our lives. To read about a new technique is one thing, putting it into practice is another.

So when I came to meditation, creative visualisation, hypnosis, energy techniques and many of the other tools that I've covered in this book, I embraced them fully, and I believe that this is why I've seen such great results. Not all of the modalities that I've tried in my life have worked for me, but I've still fully committed to them for a period of time. I became my own scientist. I'm the type of person that needs results. I don't want to theorise and pontificate, I want to see real outcomes in the real world. And to be honest, I think most people are the same.

Yet so many of the folk I meet are quick to say, *"Oh yes, I tried that and it didn't work for me."* When I ask them how long they tried it for, they say, *"Oh a few days/weeks."* This isn't enough time for the shoots of new possibility to push through fertile soil. When we give up too soon we literally miss the miracle that was about to unfold.

So, as we round up the week, I want to get you *committed* to this whole energy thing, because when you do, it'll change your life.

I'm about to share with you a daily energy practice that will ensure you have a renewed sense of energy, vitality and passion. It will also help clear the fog from your mind so that you can connect further with your inner guide and the Divine.

But in order to see any result at all, I need your commitment. But remember, you are not committing to me, you are committing to yourself.

What I'm about to share with you is a mix between Donna Eden's *Energy Medicine* and the traditional Chinese practice of *qigong*.

My clients often recommend books to me, and I always add them to my *'Must Read'* list on my office pin board. One client in passing suggested I should read Donna Eden's *'Energy Medicine For Women'*. But for whatever reason, instead of making a note of it, I went straight online and bought a copy. Clearly I was tuned into my inner guidance that day, because that simple action was to change the course of my life. I was fascinated by the simple exercises Donna was teaching and the effect they were having on her clients and students. I decided to explore further and found out more about energy exercises, discovering *qigong* in the process. I watched videos online, read books, talked to my friends and found out as much as I could about these rather bizarre energy exercises and the impact they have on the body and mind.

I decided I would put them to the test.

I found a few simple exercises that I felt would benefit me personally and made a commitment to add them to my daily practice.

I was prepared to commit to a 30-day trial period, but within just 24 hours I felt a deep shift in my energy. For the first time in months, I was buzzing with positive energy. I didn't seem to have my afternoon energy lull, I didn't crave sugar to give me a boost and I got so much more work done. I felt I could think more clearly and articulate myself better, too. To be honest, I couldn't quite believe that this had anything to do with the new exercises I was doing. After all, I had only done them once. Instead, I put it down to just having a good day.

But the next morning, I started my day off in the same way and experienced the same outcome. I did everything with more ease, and my writing flowed. I felt more balanced and calm and so much happier as a result. It was only then that I conceded that this must have something to do with the new energy exercises. I was super excited. Within just a few weeks, I was experiencing some big shifts in my life and business. Things were progressing and moving forward effortlessly. I was getting better ideas and finding solutions to problems that had been blocking me for years.

My energy was flowing freely and in response, my life was starting to flow with greater ease. *I was blown away.*

Nowadays, my energy exercises are so important to my overall wellbeing. They keep my energy system moving and healthy. When I miss a day, I certainly feel a significant difference. My children also do energy exercises before they leave for school and my husband does them in the car on his way to work. Even my mum and sister have adopted them into their practice, too. And of course, I tell all my clients to do the same.

I am a teacher and my purpose is to communicate with the world. So when I find something that works, I want to shout it from the rooftops.

So let me tell you a little more about both *qigong* and *energy medicine,* and how you can adopt these modalities to help you get your energy flowing.

Qigong and Energy Medicine

Qigong, often spelt *chi kung*, is a powerful type of health exercise, which has been practised for centuries by millions of Chinese people. It's based on the repetition of a very precise set of movements, specifically designed to benefit health on many different levels. It's easy to learn and even a few minutes spent on it a day can have an invigorating and rejuvenating effect.

Regular practice has a deep, strengthening effect on the whole body and its various systems (nervous, digestive, respiratory, skeletal-muscular, hormonal, gynaecological, etc.). The aim of qigong is to promote the movement of qi (energy) in the body. A key point in qigong practice is relaxation and deep breathing, both of which are prerequisites for allowing qi to flow.

Energy medicine is very similar in that it brings vitality, joy and zest to your mind, body and spirit. Taking care of your energies balances your body's chemistry; it regulates your hormones and helps you feel better and think more clearly. It can be used to overcome illness, change your mindset, provide a boost of physical energy and keep you strong and resilient. Energy is the medicine of the future, and the more people who know about it, the better.

Qigong and *energy medicine* both get vital life-force energy flowing through your body. They straighten out your meridians, cleanse your chakras and fill your auric field with vital energy.

And when energy is flowing, you are connected to the Divine and you feel AWESOME!

So today I'm going to teach you some energy exercises that have made a *significant* difference in my life. Use these daily and you will keep energy flowing freely around your body, helping you to feel more alive and connected.

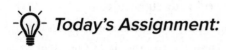 *Today's Assignment:*

Here are four simple exercises for you to try.

1) The chest tap

This exercise literally jump-starts your energy system. It flips your meridians so that they are flowing in the right direction, and it focuses your mind and gives you a boost of energy when you're feeling tired.

1. To begin, tap your chest firmly around about where a man wears the knot of his tie.
2. Tap for about 20 seconds while breathing in and out deeply. This is my favourite exercise. I tap away all day long, especially when I'm feeling low in energy.

2) The daily pat

This is to simulate your energy and immune system. It will *straighten out* and *strengthen* your meridians and clear any energy blocks.

1. Raise your left hand straight out in front of you.
2. Now use it to pat your opposite arm firmly, working your way up and down it. Swap arms. Hold your right arm out straight and use your left hand to pat it firmly.
3. Hold your left arm straight out to the side. Use your right hand to pat down the left side of your body, starting under your armpit and working down towards your hip. Switch

arms and do the same on your right side.

3. Now, using both hands, pat your stomach, hips and the outside of your legs. Then pat the inside of your legs and finally pat your bottom.
4. Pat your cheeks, forehead and the back of your neck.
5. Finish by massaging both ears firmly.

3) The connection

This exercise *opens you up* to the Divine Infinite Intelligence and *strengthens* your connection. Great for when you're feeling overwhelmed, stressed or lonely. It can also be used to bring healing energy to a particular part of your body.

1. Standing upright, connect with your breath. Bring your hands into a prayer position. Continue to focus on your breath. Now raise your hands and open your arms as if you were worshiping the sky above you. Feel the heavenly support that is greeting you. All the energy that you need is there for you to take.
2. Stay in this position for as long as you need. When you're ready, scoop the energy from the air above you into your hands, before bringing them together over your heart chakra. This brings Divine energy directly into your heart and energy system. Breathe it in. If you would prefer to take the energy to a different part of your body, that's absolutely fine.

4) Stress point

This exercise *releases tension* from your body and mind when you're feeling stressed out and down in the dumps. It reduces anxiety and helps you think more clearly, and feel calmer. You can do this on yourself, a loved one, or even a pet.

1. Sit down and relax your body. Tune into the unwanted emotion you're experiencing.
2. Now place your thumbs at your temple and the pads of your fingers on your forehead, just above your eyes.
3. Hold this point for a few minutes while focusing on your stress or emotion. Breathe in and out deeply. Continue until you notice the negative emotion reduce in intensity.

These are just four basic energy exercises that I love to use. I also encourage you to go online and type in *'energy medicine'* or *'qigong'* to find out more about different exercises and what suits you best. Or visit www.gameoflife.co.uk/latest-book/ for my demonstration of these practices.

Day 35 – Your Day For Reflection And Rest

Take time today to let what you have learned this week sink in.

Also, take a couple of minutes to answer the following questions:

1) What *insights* have you gained about yourself this week?
2) What have you *discovered* about yourself that you weren't aware of before?
3) How are you *feeling* about what you have learned?
4) How might this *change* your life for the better?
5) What is the *most important* thing that you must now do?

Prayer for this week:

"Dear Divine Guidance, thank you for helping me to release any blocked energy in my body right now, and for showing me how to raise my own natural vibrations. Show me the activities that will help me live in the flow of life. Thank you for helping me to strengthen my intuition and follow my internal guidance. Surround my home, my loved ones and me with only the highest vibrations of love today."

And so it is.

WEEK 6

DAYS 36-40

Mastering Love

Days 36-40

Mastering Love

Few people truly love themselves. In fact, many don't even like themselves very much. A huge proportion of the population spend their entire lives putting themselves down. We all do this to some degree. Maybe we do it when we look in the mirror, or walk into a meeting, or are about to go on a date. Our inner critic is always waiting in the wings to remind us how useless, unattractive, uneducated, weak or insignificant we are.

Often you will find that your inner critic is heightened just at that point when you are about to step out of your comfort zone and make a change in your life.

As a coach and mentor, I have come to realise just how *little* self-esteem people have. This only becomes an issue when we allow our lack of self-worth to impinge on the decisions we make in life. When we fail to truly accept ourselves for who we are we take fewer social, academic and career risks. But remember, everything you attract into your life is a reflection of what you feel you deserve: your job, your relationship, your home, and so on.

Don't be fooled. Loving yourself *isn't* egotistical or big-headed - that's a fallacy. In actual fact, loving yourself is *extremely healthy,* and those who do are much happier than those who don't. This isn't to do with arrogance, it's to do with having a healthy self-respect for yourself. People who hold positive beliefs about themselves attract more good into their lives: more opportunities, more money, more luck and more love.

In short, high levels of self-worth, self-esteem and confidence are vital to a happy, successful and fulfilling life.

Part of the journey towards mastering your life involves mastering self-love and accepting that you are perfect *just the way you are.* Now I know you've heard this all before, but seriously, if you don't truly love yourself, if you're constantly putting yourself down and doubting yourself, it is going to impact your goals and dreams. You might be putting your intentions out there to the Divine, but if internally you're saying to yourself, *"I don't deserve this"* or *"I'm not good enough to have this",* you will sabotage your efforts. It's that simple. Self-love really matters!

Over the last decade, I've been on a remarkable journey towards greater awareness and self-love. I have discovered new things about myself, reprogrammed my mind with new beliefs, and I have adopted countless new behaviours and habits. I have become so much more grateful to be alive. I see the awe and beauty in things, which I would have previously missed. And it feels awesome to be able to stand in my own power. I am committed to teaching others how to truly fall in love with who they are and become the happiest person they know. This is my wish for you.

So, on this final week together we'll be focusing our attention on self-care, confidence building, setting solid boundaries and becoming more appreciative.

This may be the final week of your journey, but there is still work to do.

Day 36

Is all about *self-nurturing* and learning to take care of your *own needs*. I will be showing you how to create your personal self-care manifesto.

Day 37

It's time to *boost your self-esteem* and confidence. I'll be sharing one of the most powerful exercises that I do with my private clients to increase their confidence.

Day 38

We are going to *get clear on your personal boundaries*, and I'm going to be helping you to set some solid limits in each area of your life.

Day 39

We'll be looking into *appreciation* and how creating a very simple new daily habit can bring much more joy and peace into your life.

Day 40

This is our final day together and I'll be sharing a *closing prayer* with you to assist you on your continuing journey.

Day 36 - Falling In Love With You!

Today, we are focusing on *self-care*, which involves taking care of yourself emotionally, physically and spiritually. This is important because not doing so affects your energy systems and your ability to co-create with the Divine. Most of us feel guilty when it comes to spending time and money on ourselves. We are all blighted by the G word. If we're not careful guilt can consume us, sap our energy and steal away happiness.

We all have commitments, obligations and responsibilities that we can't ignore. I have to wipe my kids' snotty noses, walk my dog, Max, clean my toilets and see my clients. But I know that if I don't take a little time out each day or week I quickly become unbalanced. And I'm not a happy bunny when I'm unbalanced and my energy is low. Just ask my husband.

Also, when you don't value and take care of your own needs you give a mixed message to the Divine. On one hand you're saying, *"I want this,"* but on the other you're stating, *"I don't matter!"* Those vibrations don't match!

So many of us are givers, always running around and making sure that we keep our boss happy, that the kids have gone off to school with the right lunch box, that we've paid the telephone bill, put the bins out or phoned our mum. There is always something that diverts us away from spending time nourishing ourselves. Even if we did have a spare five minutes in our already manic schedule, most of us wouldn't have a clue what to do with it! Over time we have become accustomed to our frighteningly fast pace of life. The TV, internet and our smart phones all play a part in stealing our attention away from ourselves. We collapse in front of the TV each night with a glass of red to help us unwind and relax. It's a vicious circle. Before we know it, another week has gone by and we have still haven't found the time to shave our legs or phone the hairdresser to book our next appointment.

It's time to slow down and recognise our own needs.
This is a must.

We talked earlier about your daily practice and spending time in your energy vortex. This is self-nurturing and vitally important. But today, I want to talk to you about physically taking care of yourself; giving yourself treats that show you matter. When you nurture yourself this way, it gives a clear message that you are important. You'll notice that other people will respond to this and start treating you with the love and respect you deserve.

I remember when I started taking an interest in raw food and experimenting with juicing and blending. I was moaning to my coach about how expensive organic fruit and veg was, and carping on about how my shopping bill had gone up by £30 every week.

She laughed and explained that while on one hand I was asking for more abundance from the Universe, on the other I was saying that I didn't value myself enough to spend a few extra quid each week nurturing my body with health foods. Hmmmmm, now this really made me sit up and realise that I was clearly giving off a mixed message. Of course my family and I were worth an extra £30. And while it might be a good idea to spend a little extra on healthier foods, a holistic or beauty treatment, or a sparkly new top, there are many things that we can do to nurture ourselves that cost *nothing*.

Money or no money, there are a myriad of ways in which we can take better care of ourselves. When we do this, we feel so much brighter. We're more contented and therefore attract more abundance into our lives.

Think of it like this. You have £100 in your bank. If you keep giving away £10 here and there without replenishing it, you'll end up skint. There is no money in the bank. You have to fill up your reserves, whether that's physically, energetically, emotionally or spiritually. *You have to keep putting fuel in your tank or you simply won't go.*

Today, we are going to create a self-care manifesto

Every January, I create my own *self-care manifesto*. I thought I'd share with you just some of the things that are on my list this year:

- ★ Take myself to lunch with my favourite magazine.
- ★ Go for a walk in nature by myself.
- ★ Lie on my sofa with my Kindle.
- ★ Sit in the garden with a cup of tea.
- ★ Have a Sunday morning lie-in.
- ★ Go shopping and treat myself to something special.
- ★ Grow something in the garden.
- ★ Take an Epsom salt bath with candles.
- ★ Paint my nails.
- ★ Go on a retreat.
- ★ Go to yoga weekly.
- ★ Buy gorgeous new makeup.

With two young children and a business to run, life can be rather hectic and some days I find it hard to get a minute to myself. So each week I make an appointment with myself, no matter *how* busy I am. I get my nails done, or I take time to read a novel or enjoy an afternoon nap. Each week, I pick something from my self-care manifesto and use it to nurture myself. This is *non-negotiable.*

It's time for you to do the same. Drop the guilt (yes, I can hear your inner critic screaming that you haven't got the time, money, energy, and so on). I am giving you full permission.

Now you must give yourself full permission to nurture and pamper yourself. You need it!

Answer the following questions to help you think about how you're going to look after yourself better:

1) Where do I feel deprived?
2) What do I need more of right now?
3) What am I yearning for?
4) Who are the people in my life that nourish me?
5) What places or locations nourish me?
6) What activities nourish me?
7) What thoughts nourish me?

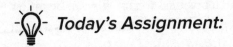 *Today's Assignment:*

You are going to create a self-care manifesto.

List the things that you can do for yourself (free or paid for) that will make you *feel good*. This could be spending an afternoon in the park, reading a book, taking a long bath, cooking, gardening, dancing, and so on. Write down whatever makes your spirit soar and puts you in a state of flow. Put your list up someplace where you'll see it often.

Now here's the important part:

Make an appointment with yourself *each week* to pick something from your self-care manifesto to do. Remember, the more nourished you are, the more *connected* you will be with the Divine. Find just an hour a week (or more) to nourish yourself in whatever way feels right for you.

Write it in your diary or on your calendar if necessary (this is what I do).

Give yourself permission to spend a little time taking care
of you and see what difference it makes to the way
you feel at the end of the week.

Day 37 – Phone A Friend

Learning to accept and love yourself isn't easy. It only takes one set back to allow your inner critic to wade in and remind you how stupid, unattractive or uneducated you are. If you're not careful, your old programming will pop up to sabotage your efforts.

We are our own *worst* critics. We look in the mirror and scowl at our reflection, we chastise ourselves when we make a mistake and we put ourselves down when talking to friends. In truth, we're not particularly nice to ourselves. We wouldn't dare treat our friends the way we treat ourselves.

I have often fallen into the trap of *compare and despair*. And I have been on the edge of a major breakthrough and found myself sabotaging all my hard work. And the crazy thing is, I know I'm doing it, but I just can't seem to stop myself. The thing about being too focused on where you're going is that it's very easy to forget where you've been, and just how awesome you actually are. We are quick to highlight our own flaws, yet forget our successes far too readily.

I often get clients to stop and listen to their internal dialogue, and to what their inner critic is saying to them in different areas of their lives: work, home, dating, food, and so on. The negative barrage of abuse that washes through their minds each day, or spills out of their mouths, always amazes clients. This negative self-talk is an indicator that there are still some limiting beliefs at play which need to be cleared out for good.

As we near the end of our time together, I want to share with you a *powerful* gem that has turned out to be one of the most successful exercises that my clients have undertaken while working with me. I use this exercise in many different circumstances and it really shows us truths that we often can't see for ourselves.

It's Time to Phone a Friend

I'd like to set you a practical assignment today to list five people who you trust and respect. Make sure that they are from different areas of your life. They could be a family member, a friend, a work colleague, an associate or a social contact. Select wisely and pick people who you value and admire.

At this stage you might be feeling a little nervous about asking these people for their feedback. Don't worry because you will be only be asking them to talk about the stuff they love about you. No negatives allowed. You must state this clearly to them.

In *Today's Assignment* is a list of suggested questions that I'd like you to ask each of the people on your list. I recommend that you meet or talk on the phone with each person beforehand to explain the context of the exercise, and then either ask your questions verbally or over email.

Rightly or wrongly, we live in a society where other people's opinions affect our self-esteem and confidence. Sometimes it takes someone else to say something positive before we can believe it for ourselves.

This feedback is *powerful ammunition* for you to finally combat your inner critic.

Rachel was a client that I worked with a few years ago. She was a 29-year-old Londoner, was single and in a job that totally sapped her energy. Together, we worked on her big goal to launch a new business and leave the confines of the corporate 9 to 5 world behind for good. As we progressed, I noticed that Rachel's lack of self-belief was affecting her progress. Every time she took a step forward she would sabotage her efforts. I decided that it was time for her to *phone a friend.* She was quite resistant to begin with, as she felt is was somewhat self-centred to ask friends for feedback on what they loved about her. But despite her reservations, she gave it a go. She was surprised at how willing friends and family were to answer her questions. And the feedback that came back was life changing for Rachel.

When do we ever question our parents about what they love about us? When do we ask our mates to say what they value most about our friendship, or work colleagues to say what they feel our gifts are? Rachel's feedback blew her away because she received such positive words of love and encouragement. This changed everything for her, and her self-belief soared. Yes, she still had wobbles, but on those days she'd stop and pull out her phone a friend exercise. This would empower her enough to take the next step.

By completing today's exercise, you will get some really good insights into your qualities and gifts. More often than not, you'll receive valuable information on the attributes that you didn't even know you had!

So here we go.

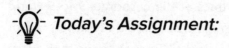 *Today's Assignment:*

List five or more people that you would like to make contact with.

Remember to choose carefully.

Send them the following questions and ask them to give you the answers by a specific date:

1) What do you perceive to be my greatest strengths?
2) What do you like most about me?
3) What do you value most about me?
4) What three words sum up the positive points about me?
5) When in my life have you really seen me shine?
6) What would you call me to help you with?

After you have received all of the feedback, reflect on what has been written or said:

➢ How do you feel about it?
➢ Are there any surprises?
➢ Do you feel confident about your abilities?
➢ How can you use this information to go forward?
➢ If these people believe that you have these strengths then so do a lot of others, too – how does that make you feel?
➢ What key insights have you gained?

Day 38 - Set Those Boundaries

You've all heard the word *boundary* and have an idea of what it means, but how many of you are aware of your personal boundaries in life? And how many of you fully realise how weak boundaries affect your power to co-create?

My definition of a boundary is this: '*A boundary is simply something that indicates a border or a limit; it's a separation between you and me and it helps you to decide what you will and won't do.*'

Of course, boundaries can alter with various people and be adjusted in different situations. We have different boundaries with different people. Just think of the borders between different countries. Some have very relaxed measures with no checks, and some have barbed wire and soldiers patrolling the parameter.

We are more likely to invite the people we care about the most, such as our children and partner, deep into our emotional and physical space. We tend to be more willing to make compromises for them. And it's these individuals that are more likely to *breach* our personal boundaries. When it's someone we've met just the once, our boundaries are likely to be more rigid. We wouldn't generally invite someone we didn't know to sit down with us and ask intimate personal questions. Boundaries can be elastic, shifting to fit what we need at the time, and dependent on how strong or vulnerable we happen to feel.

For example, the boundaries I have with my kids may differ to the boundaries of another parent. Professionally my boundaries may be firmer or weaker than those of another mentor or coach. Our energy system is very aware of how close we want to let someone get to us on a physical, emotional, mental or energetic level. Our vibes let us know when something doesn't feel good, or when someone has crossed a boundary that we're not comfortable with.

For example, having lovely neighbours is great. You can chat and provide a cup of sugar in times of need. But having a fence to separate your personal living space is great, too. This way you don't cross the boundary and encroach on each other's vital space. This boarder makes for a more peaceful and harmonious relationship all round. It keeps things healthy.

Yet many of us have terribly weak boundaries when it comes to our love life, our work, children, self-care, and so on. Weak boundaries mean leaky energy! You cannot shine your light fully if you keep giving it away. People will take from you, and although energy exchange is natural, some people take way more than they need. Keeping your boundaries firm will enable you to be loving and giving, but also stand firm in your own power. When you can do this you become a much better co-creator.

It's nice to be needed. It's lovely to be the person that people go to when they need a shoulder to cry on, but it's not so nice when your phone is constantly ringing with friends wanting to sap your energy. If you find that you are overrun with doing stuff for other people, or are carrying other's problems around, it's a clear sign that you need to put some solid boundaries in place.

Weak boundaries are sometimes just habitual behavioural patterns that we've adopted as we've grown up. We saw our mother constantly backing down and giving in to our father and adopted the same pattern of behaviour as a result.

More often than not, weak boundaries are due to some underlying limiting belief that is running beneath the surface. We let people take from us and cross the boundary line because on some level we want them to like or love us. But if we're not careful, weak boundaries can leave us feeling burnt-out, frustrated and resentful. We end up feeling used because we are getting little in return. As I said, energy exchange is natural, but it's only positive when energy is being exchanged from both parties equally.

Let me give you a couple of examples to illustrate weak boundaries.

1) *My son has a powerful energy field.* He's extremely sensitive and loving, but he also has a needy side, which can be exhausting. He's a full on type of child. He knows what he wants, and if getting it means pushing other people's boundaries, he will. He's constantly waiting in the wings for our boundaries to slip so that he can pounce. Just one late night, half an hour extra on his computer game, or a sweetie before dinner causes the boundaries to become blurred, and he starts to feel out of balance. We very quickly have to reinforce the boundaries before he takes it too far.

Most kids need firm boundaries, but my son needs super tight parameters. When his boundaries are firm, he's a happier child and everyone knows where they stand.

2) *In the early days of my business, as I was trying to establish myself as a coach, I would often work all hours.* If a client wanted a session on a Sunday afternoon, I'd do it. If a client wanted to meet face-to-face, I'd drive 60 miles to see them. I had no idea about

boundaries and I burnt myself out trying to please everyone as a result. The more I offered, the more my clients took. Thankfully, this didn't last long. I realised that if I didn't take care of myself, I wouldn't be much use to anyone else. I set some firm business boundaries. I decided that if clients wanted to meet me face-to-face, they would have to see me at my choice of location. I vowed to only work certain days and hours, and I also put limits on the number of clients I worked with at any one time.

Balance was restored and what a relief that was!

This is about standing in your own power. People really respect this. It's a high vibrational frequency that *feels good*. You can still be loving and caring, but be firm at the same time. Establishing boundaries makes our interactions smoother, more comfortable and safe.

So, we're going to firm up your boundaries so that you can stand in your own power and shine your light fully.

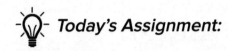 *Today's Assignment:*

Take a look at the following areas of your life and list all the boundaries that you need to start putting in place.

I've come up with some suggested ones, but feel free to create your own.

Romantic relationships

- ➢ I will not be belittled.
- ➢ I will not accept cheating.
- ➢ I will not allow physical or mental abuse.

Work

- ➢ I will not put up with a member of my team turning up consistently late for meetings.
- ➢ I will not be put down by anyone.
- ➢ I will not work weekends.

Children

- ➢ I will not accept answering back.
- ➢ I will not tolerate hitting or being mean to a sibling.
- ➢ I will not accept swearing.

Family and friends

- ➢ I will not accept talking behind my back.
- ➢ I will not tolerate a lack of support.
- ➢ Stealing from me is unacceptable.

Personal/Self-care

- ➢ I will get seven hours sleep each night.
- ➢ I will meditate daily.
- ➢ I will put aside money for my self-nurturing.
- ➢ I will ensure I shave my legs before a date.
- ➢ I will eat my five-a-day.

At Home

- ➢ I will keep my house tidy.
- ➢ I will not take work calls at home.
- ➢ I will shut down my computer at 9.00pm.
- ➢ I will take at least half an hour to wind down before bed.

Day 39 – Thank You God!

We've almost come to the end of our journey together, and today is your *last assignment* – it's an important one!

I have shared many tools and modalities throughout this book to help you master your life. But there is one topic that I have deliberately left until the end.

And that is *appreciation*.

This really is the driving force for creating the life you want.
An appreciative heart can create miracles and
change the world.

Too many people are stuck in undesirable circumstances because of lack of *gratitude*. When you are not thankful for all that you have, you cut the wires that connect you to the Divine Infinite Intelligence.

I know that life can sometimes throw us a curveball, and I know that it sucks when we haven't got enough money coming in to pay the bills. I'm also aware that it's heartbreaking to be cast aside in love, or fail at something we've been working hard at. But despite the challenges that life sometimes throws us, we must look for the good that lies beneath. There is a reason for everything; that I am sure of. The Divine matrix is unfathomable and miraculous. Our job is to hold on tight and stay connected. Appreciation keeps us connected and strong when we feel like life is just too damned hard.

When we are appreciative in life, more miracles come, we are more aligned with the Divine and our lives change faster.

Appreciation keeps us focused on the whole and prevents us from falling into *victim* mode and believing that supply is limited in life. This kind of limited thinking is death to our goals and dreams. When we allow our thoughts to fall into the trap of compare and despair, we slow down our creative power to manifest. We lose ground and everything grinds to a halt.

> *An appreciative mind is always looking for the silver*
> *lining and the good in any person or situation.*
> *She expects good things to come her way.*

So it's necessary to cultivate a grateful mind. In fact, *it's imperative.*

We must notice when our thoughts have turned sour, or when we're becoming too absorbed in our own shortcomings. In this moment of shifting our awareness, we regain our power.

When I was 29, I had a terrible miscarriage that almost cost me my life. The loss of our unborn baby was terribly difficult, and I struggled to understand why this had happened to me. I was heartbroken, and it took me many months to regain my physical and emotional strength. My faith had also been wobbled to the core. Why had the Universe let this happen? At that point, I didn't feel like being appreciative for anything. I was angry. I was grieving for what we had lost. After a few months of feeling very low, I finally turned a corner. I decided that I had had enough of being a victim and moping around feeling sorry for myself. It was time to regain my power and get back on track. I came to the conclusion that bad things happen to good people sometimes, and maybe I would never get to fully understand why. I turned my focus to gratitude and started to keep a regular diary, listing all the things that I had appreciated during the day: the weather, the dustbin men for taking my rubbish, Tetley tea, my bed, my glasses, and so on.

Some days my list was very short indeed, on others I could easily fill a page. But over the weeks that followed I started to notice some remarkable changes. Instead of scanning the world for all the bad stuff, I was consciously starting to look for nice things to appreciate. And I was doing this without really thinking about it. One morning, I marvelled at a flock of starlings as they swooped and swished across the sky. I realised in that moment that maybe life wasn't all that bad after all. I found myself appreciating the things that people did for me in a way that I hadn't done before. I woke up in the morning feeling thankful for my life and the day ahead. My thinking had changed and I was feeling so much brighter and happier as a result. I keep a gratitude journal to this day. It keeps my vibes high and helps me to stay focused and positive. And what's really fabulous about actually writing these things down is that when you do have a bad day, or your confidence gets knocked, you can pick up your journal, read a few pages and feel awesome and grateful again.

When you are conscious about gratitude you start scanning the world in a different way.

You look for all the good stuff instead of all the bad. This is a humongous shift in your thinking. Gratitude rewires your brain.

Obviously, I'm all for focusing on dreams and setting big goals because it makes life exciting and brings amazing things our way. But having said this, it's also important to be content and present, because if we're not, life can pass us by. When we're too focused on where we're going we can miss the beauty of the present moment. If we are always waiting for some future event to happen in order to feel happy or fulfilled, we are not experiencing life as we should.

> *We are present when we are being grateful, and magic happens when we're in the moment.*

So, on this final day, I want you to start your own *gratitude journal*. Alternatively, you might prefer to call it something else such as, *'Things to be appreciative about'*, *'My thank you book'* or *'Best thing about today.'*

Each day, write down at least five things that you have appreciated, from stroking your dog on the sofa, to hanging washing on the line in your garden. Look for the small things, the things that generally go unnoticed and unappreciated.

Remember, when you do this you are rewiring your brain and programming it to look for the good. The more good stuff you notice, the more you'll see.

Try it, it's life changing!

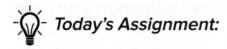 *Today's Assignment:*

Start a Gratitude Journal.

Buy yourself a pretty little notebook and give it a name. Find a place for it in your home: your bedside table, your coffee table, by your kettle or in your energy vortex space. Fill it in *each day* with things that you've noticed and are *grateful* for. This will keep your vibration high and ensure that you are connected and happy.

Also, give this super quick exercise by Donna Eden a try. It will help you to retain a feeling of gratitude for far longer. This is because it trains the nervous system to bring in more feelings of joy. The good moments in your life will be imprinted on your mind, and you'll see the positive more readily.

Here's what to do.

1. Firstly, bring something to mind that you feel really grateful for, or just a really happy memory.
2. Now tap your third eye, which is in between your eyebrows, with your middle finger for about 10 seconds. This literally taps the feeling into the first acupuncture point on your nervous system, and that helps to rewire your brain. Just tap for 10 seconds while focusing on a happy thought. As you do this, know that you are firing up new positive neural pathways in your brain.

You can also tap in positive affirmations such as: *"My life gets more fabulous every day. I look forward to what each new hour brings."*

Day 40 – Your Day For Reflection and Rest

Take time today to let what you have learned this week sink in.

Also take a couple of minutes to answer the following questions:

1) What *insights* have you gained about yourself this week?
2) What have you *discovered* about yourself that you weren't aware of before?
3) How are you *feeling* about what you have learned?
4) How might this *change* your life for the better?
5) What is the most *important* thing that you must now do?

Prayer For This Week:

"Dear Divine Guidance, although I might sometimes not value or love myself, I ask for your help to see myself the way you made me, beautiful and perfect - just as I am. I am willing to release all self-limiting beliefs and accept myself as I am. I am enough. Please guide my thoughts towards love, peace and gratitude."

And so it is.

Final Reflection On Your 40-day Miracle Masterplan

So there you have it, we have come to the end of your 40-day Miracle Masterplan. I hope you have enjoyed the journey and are putting into practice many of the ideas, tips, suggestions and practices that I have shared over the last six weeks.

I would like to acknowledge you for getting this far, for your openness, willingness and courage to go the distance. Well done. The most important thing you can do now is to stay connected to your inner guide and the Divine. When you're connected you get everything you need. And of course, let's not forget action! You must not forget to take action. Connection and action is all you truly need.

I want to share some very important words of wisdom with you before we part company. It's short and sweet, but it needs to be said.

Creating a beautiful life isn't always easy and plain sailing. There will be amazing highs and also profound lows. Sometimes those 6am beeps from your alarm clock will seem like the worst idea you've ever had. Sometimes you won't want to switch on your computer or make that phone call. Sometimes your trainers will seem like the living incarnation of evil. Sometimes you will question what the hell you're doing. Someone you will feel abandoned by your inner guide. You will cry - lots. Sometimes your mind will play tricks on you. Sometimes you will shake with fear. And sometimes you will just want to jack it all in and reclaim your old comfortable life back.

This is life.

But let me tell you something I wished I had known at the beginning of my journey. The discomfort of change is only temporary. Everything in life is transitory and everything eventually passes. Just feel the burn and let it pass.

This is life.

Enjoy your ride, because it's your unique journey. Open your eyes, smile, take in the view, feel the wind in your hair, squeeze the hand of the person next to you and scream at the top of your lungs if necessary.

This is YOUR life.

And most importantly, remember that the burn means you are getting closer.

Keep the burn going and don't ever stop.

With love

Your coach

Louise

Louise x

Below is a list of *really important questions* to help you reflect on your journey so far. Remember, your journey is not over; there is always more to come!

Please take time to answer these questions thoroughly.

1) What have you *achieved* in the last 40 days that makes you feel proud?
2) How can you *continue* to build on this success?
3) What do you *need* to do more of?
4) How has the Divine *shown up* in your life? Have you experienced chance meetings, inspired ideas, timely emails, and so on?
5) What have been your *biggest challenges* and how did you overcome them?
6) What has been your *biggest discovery* about yourself during the last 40 days?
7) How are you *feeling?*
8) What will you do *differently* that you didn't do before?
9) What is your *greatest desire* for the future?
10) What is the most important thing that you must now *do* in order to continue to create miracles in your life?

About Louise

Personal Growth Expert, Author, Speaker and Business Mentor.

Louise's expertise and life changing techniques have secured her position as one of the UK's most prolific personal growth experts. She helps women to find their purpose and create an awesome life on their own terms.

Louise has featured in many top national magazines and newspapers, and on BBC Radio. She also writes regular blogs for *The Huffington Post*. Her unique style of coaching has produced some amazing results, helping people to define their goals and turn their lives around.

Louise is also the founder of *International Change Your Life Week,* a free initiative that allows anyone access to expert help and advice in all areas of their lives.

Want More?

To join Louise's mailing list and get your free meditation download and life planner log on to:
www.thegameoflife.co.uk

For further details on workshops, retreats, online courses, corporate work and media requests just visit:
www.thegameoflife.co.uk

If you'd like to work with Louise privately, then contact her team now at:
info@thegameoflife.co.uk

Notes

Notes

Notes

Notes

Notes

Notes